-THE-
CHINESE
PEOPLE
STAND UP

ELIZABETH WRIGHT

26/00/89

FOR MY PARENTS

ACKNOWLEDGEMENTS

Over the years, the number of people who have helped me to form my views on China
are too many to name, but the Chinese people themselves must come top of any list.
In the academic field I would like to thank the sinologists at Harvard University
(especially Professor Roderick MacFarquhar), Columbia University and the
University of Michigan in the United States. In Britain, Dr Jonathan Mirsky,
Dr Cyril Lin and Dr Elisabeth Croll all gave advice and encouragement.
In the BBC, Sam Younger, head of Current Affairs World Service in English not
only gave birth to the idea of the book and the radio series, but also gave me three and
a half months away from the BBC in order to write the book. My colleague, Simon
Long of the BBC's Far Eastern Service, was invaluable in checking and evaluating the
manuscript and making very useful suggestions and corrections. But my warmest
thanks must go to my friend and colleague David Powell, the Producer of the radio
series of the same title. If this book has any merit at all, it is because of his trenchant
comments on the first draft. I am also most grateful to Jeremy Polmear for having
de-mystified word-processing and so speeded up the actual writing, and to my father
as an indefatigable collector of newspaper cuttings.

PICTURE ACKNOWLEDGEMENTS

page i main picture Xinhua Press Agency, inset Weidenfeld (publishers) Ltd; ii top
Hulton-Deutsch Collection, bottom Fairbank, John K. & Feurwerker, Albert (Eds)
The Cambridge History of China vol 13, pt 2, CUP (1986), p. 210; iii top woodcut by
Lia Hua, 1950, bottom Xinhua; iv top Mo Ce, British Library, bottom Hulton-
Deutsch Collection, inset SACU; v top SACU, bottom A.P.; vi top Xinhua, bottom
SACU; vii top SACU, bottom Xinhua; viii main picture and inset A.P.; ix Xinhua; x
top and bottom right S. & R. Greenhill; xi top and bottom
S. & R. Greenhill; xii top Xinhua, bottom S. & R. Greenhill; xiii all S. & R. Greenhill;
xiv–xvi all A.P.

COVER: A.P.

ABBREVIATIONS:
SACU = Society for Anglo-Chinese Understanding
A.P. = Associated Press

Published by BBC Books,
A Division of BBC Enterprises Ltd
Woodlands, 80 Wood Lane, London W12 0TT

First published 1989

© Elizabeth Wright 1989

ISBN 0 563 207620

Typeset in 11/12 pt Bodoni by Goodfellow & Egan Phototypesetting Ltd
Printed and bound in Great Britain by Mackays of Chatham Ltd
Cover printed by Richard Clay Ltd, Norwich

CONTENTS

PREFACE   4

A NOTE ON CHINESE PROPER NAMES   4

BRIEF CHRONOLOGY OF IMPORTANT
DATES   5

CHAPTER ONE
THE CHINESE PEOPLE STAND UP   6

CHAPTER TWO
A FRAGILE UNITY   28

CHAPTER THREE
THE CULTURAL REVOLUTION   52

CHAPTER FOUR
DEATH OF AN EMPEROR   87

CHAPTER FIVE
REFORM WITHOUT DEMOCRACY   112

CHAPTER SIX
CHINA'S PLACE IN THE WORLD   164

EPILOGUE   201

INDEX   207

PREFACE

This is not a book for China experts. It was written to accompany the BBC World Service and Radio 4 series of the same name, and is intended to give the general reader an overall picture of China's political, economic and social development over the past forty years. To understand how the Communist Party came to establish the People's Republic of China on 1 October 1949, it is important to know the background to the events which led to that dramatic change of government, so the first chapter is devoted to the Republican period. I have deliberately avoided details of the quarrels which took place in the Chinese Communist Party in the 1920s and 1930s, as most of the losers then disappeared from centre stage, and all the extra names would only have confused the reader. In the Epilogue, in addition to summing up China's achievements and failures on its fortieth anniversary, I have also attempted to predict what effect the violent suppression in June 1989 of the popular demonstrations in Tiananmen Square may have on the future development of China.

Elizabeth Wright

A NOTE ON CHINESE PROPER NAMES

I have been quite arbitrary in my choice of spellings of proper names, and have generally opted for the version with which the reader may be more familiar. Thus, I have chosen Peking, rather than Beijing, and Canton, rather than Guangzhou. Sun Yat-sen and Chiang Kai-shek have not been converted into the Pinyin version of romanisation, whereas Mao Zedong (Mao Tse-tung) and Zhou Enlai (Chou En-lai) have. I made my choices in an attempt to obviate confusion, rather than to cause it!

BRIEF CHRONOLOGY
OF IMPORTANT DATES

1949   1 October, People's Republic of China founded.

1950–53 Korean War.

1956–57 The 'Hundred Flowers Movement' precipitates the
            Anti-Rightist Campaign.

1958   Launch of the Great Leap Forward and establish-
            ment of the communes.

1960   Split with the Soviet Union.

1966   The Cultural Revolution starts in earnest.

1971   Lin Biao, Defence Minister and Mao's chosen suc-
            cessor, reportedly attempts a coup.

1976   Zhou Enlai dies in January, and his death sparks
            the Tiananmen Incident in April. This leads to the
            disgrace of Deng Xiaoping. Mao Zedong dies in
            September. The Gang of Four are arrested in
            October.

1978   The Third Plenum of the Eleventh Central Com-
            mittee marks the launch of the economic reforms.

1986   Widespread student demonstrations at the end of
            the year lead to the forced resignation in January
            1987 of the General Secretary of the Chinese
            Communist Party, Hu Yaobang.

1989   April. The death of former Party General Secretary
            Hu Yaobang sparks off large-scale student demon-
            strations in Peking.

1989   May. Mikhail Gorbachev visits China for the first
            Sino–Soviet summit for over three decades.

1989   3–4 June. The Chinese army crushes mass demon-
            strations in Peking's Tiananmen Square.

CHAPTER ONE

THE CHINESE PEOPLE STAND UP

During the night of 3 and 4 June 1989, forces of the Chinese People's Liberation Army moved into Tiananmen Square — the Square of the Gate of Heavenly Peace — in the heart of Peking. They were there to crush the mass demonstrations which had been taking place in the centre of the city since the middle of April. The protesters had been demanding freedom of the press, greater democracy, the elimination of corruption in the Chinese Communist Party, and the resignation of certain of China's top leaders. The troops machine-gunned down unarmed student protesters, and ran their tanks over others who had been on hunger strike. In horror and disbelief, the world watched the massacre as it was broadcast by foreign television stations. It is estimated that between 700 and 3000 were killed, and thousands more were wounded.

And yet forty years ago on 1 October 1949 a tall, thickset man called Mao Zedong, had looked out over that same Square from his vantage point on the Gate of Heavenly Peace and had declared the founding of the People's Republic of China. He said 'The Chinese people have stood up'. To the vast and motley crowd who stood in the Square and witnessed that historic occasion, the feeling must have been an indescribable relief mixed with the unspoken question as to whether the years of war, turmoil, poverty and uncertainty had really come to an end. For the man gazing over the cheering crowds the triumph was no surprise, for he had always said that it would happen. But the four previous decades had been a period of constant strife, during which any but the most determined of characters would have given up hope of victory.

For Mao Zedong was born at the end of the nineteenth century, when China was still ruled by the last imperial dynasty of China, the Qing. It was weak, corrupt and crumbling under the pressures of the foreign powers. The first Opium War in the 1840s had brought China into sudden and humiliating contact with Western imperialism, and as the century progressed, the foreign powers gained a firmer foothold in China. Those foreigners whom the Chinese had despised as 'barbarians' might still be barbarians, but they now had infinitely superior firepower and technology, and the European eighteenth-century admiration of Chinese cultural and philosophical superiority had turned into nineteenth-century contempt for a people who were poor, technologically backward and 'heathen'.

Following the first Opium War a series of treaties forced on the Chinese gave the Western powers, the Soviet Union and, later, Japan an increasing hold over China. Foreigners living in the 'treaty ports' were subject to the laws of their own countries, not China's; foreign navies sailed in Chinese waters; foreign soldiers guarded foreign legations; missionaries had penetrated to the Chinese interior.

This gradual diminution of Chinese sovereignty fuelled an increasing nationalism amongst many Chinese. At the beginning of the twentieth century the Qing dynasty was ruled, to all intents and purposes, by the formidable and xenophobic Dowager Empress Ci Xi. But the Qing dynasty was itself a foreign dynasty. Its rulers were not from the majority Han Chinese race, but were Manchus from North-East China, and were disliked almost as much as the Westerners. Already by 1910 delegates from sixteen provincial assemblies had arrived in Peking to demand the formation of a parliament, and this had been promised for 1913. But in 1911 a mutiny by soldiers in central China precipitated the election of Dr Sun Yat-sen as provisional President of China's new Republic.

Sun Yat-sen's Three Principles were the mainstay of the new political philosophy. They embodied the Western concepts of nationalism, democracy and the welfare of the people. Although ill-defined and somewhat wishy-washy, they were to become the basis of Chiang Kai-shek's Nationalist Party, or Kuomintang (KMT). Ironically, Dr Sun's ideas were regarded as dangerously radical by all of the Western powers, except the Americans, so he was forced, in the early 1920s, to reorganise his Nationalist Party with the help of the Comintern,who sent Russian experts to China to advise the fledgling Party.

The rising tide of nationalism throughout China had been given further impetus by the Treaty of Versailles in 1919. As the foreign powers battled with each other in various theatres of war, so their territorial acquisitions in China came to reflect their victories and defeats. After the Russian fleet was destroyed by the Japanese in 1905, the Russians surrendered their rights and their railway in Manchuria (North-East China) to the victors, the Japanese, who were later to annexe the entire territory from China and set up their own puppet empire. At the start of the First World War the Japanese took over a German sphere of influence on China's east coast, and this was confirmed in the Treaty of Versailles. There was outrage in China that the territory was not to be returned to China, and this precipitated massive student protests.

The students, and millions around China who sympathised with them, knew that there had to be a fundamental change. They called for the eradication of traditional thinking and beliefs, fearing that otherwise an emasculated China would always be a prey to the demands of the strong foreign powers. Some advocated complete Westernisation, but others felt that this would be as ineffectual as clinging to the traditional ways. By the beginning of the 1920s another, quite unexpected solution was beginning to be considered – Marxism.

The Chinese Communist Party was founded in July 1921 in the city of Shanghai. As an insurance against prying eyes, the founders met on a boat on the Huangpu River. Of the mere dozen who started the movement which was to change the course of China's history, one was Mao Zedong. But even amongst that small number of founding members there were already differences of opinion which were to erupt cataclysmically in the years to come. An intriguing aspect of the two parties which were to become such bitter enemies over the next two decades and more – the Communists and the Nationalists – was that both were fundamentally similar in their early stages and, indeed, retained many similarities later on. Both parties regarded the tasks ahead as possible only if they had dictatorial powers. Both parties claimed legitimacy based on different combinations of nationalism and social justice. Both were revolutionary parties; both were nationalistic; both were opposed to the warlordism which was ravaging China at the time.

The appeal of a new order was considerable, except to the tiny minority which held the power and wealth of China. The hopes which accompanied the downfall of the imperial system and the establishment of the Republic were short-lived. Powerful military leaders around China used their private armies and the wealth squeezed from local taxation to wrest power from each other. These warlord armies were often little better than bandits, and the hapless Chinese were powerless as they were robbed, taxed, conscripted and even murdered.

The man who eventually emerged as the strongest of all the warlords was Chiang Kai-shek, and under him the Nationalists, or KMT, became more and more the party of the status quo. But in the early 1920s the KMT was still under the influence of the left wing, and members of the Communist Party held influential positions in the KMT. Both Mao Zedong and Zhou Enlai, later to become Prime Minister of the People's Republic of China, held posts in both parties simultaneously. At that time the ideological differences between the two parties were not great, but even if they had been, Mao would still have been prepared to engage in such united-front tactics, believing that any disputes could be addressed once they had gained joint victory. This was a tactic that Mao was to use time and time again, and it was eventually to make him the leader of all China. But even had he objected to the United Front, pressure from Stalin and the Comintern, who saw it as the Communist Party's best hope, would have forced him to swallow his doubts.

Under the leadership of Chiang Kai-shek the KMT was gradually purged of its left wing. The intellectuals who had initially been attracted by Dr Sun Yat-sen's Three Principles became more and more disillusioned with the growing militarism and authoritarianism of the KMT, and were increasingly attracted to the Communist Party.

With the death of Sun Yat-sen in 1925, Chiang Kai-shek took over the Nationalist government, then based in the southern city of Canton (Guangzhou). Mao Zedong knew that

Chiang would waste no time in moving north, mopping up recalcitrant warlords on his way; he would aim to take Peking, and try to establish KMT control over the whole of China. Chiang did indeed move north. He bought off some warlords, fought others, and set them against each other whenever he could. Meanwhile, the tensions between the KMT and the Communists were also increasing, and in April 1927, nine days after he had taken Shanghai, Chiang ordered a massacre of Communists and armed militants who had led an uprising of workers to coincide with his own attack on the city. After his victory, such people were too dangerous to be allowed to live. Although there are no definite figures for the numbers killed they ran into the hundreds, and this was a terrible blow to the urban Communist movement. Many of those who survived took to the hills, and the remainder worked underground in Shanghai, in constant danger of their lives. Some were executed, some bought their freedom, taking advantage of the corruption of their captors. But the nexus of the Communist movement had moved to the countryside, and there it was to stay until final victory in 1949.

Before looking at what was now to be open war between the Communists and the KMT, it is as well to examine the backgrounds of some of the main players in one of history's more extraordinary and protracted conflicts. There was Chiang Kai-shek, the 'Generalissimo', leader of the KMT, supported by both Stalin and the Americans. His appeal to the West lay in the fact that he was a Christian, he seemed to be the one strong figure who could unite the chaos that was then China, and, above all, he was anti-Communist. Such a man might be able to combat the Communist government in the Soviet Union.

But it is the Communist leaders who are the more relevant here, for they were the men who led China after 1949, whilst Chiang had to be content with ruling the small island of Taiwan. First amongst the Communist leaders was, of course, Mao Zedong himself. But Zhou Enlai, Liu Shaoqi, Lin Biao and now, above all, Deng Xiaoping have all entered the lexicon of history. In addition to these, there are many more, like Zhu De and Peng Dehuai, famous for their military exploits and the high prices on their heads. And there was the now notorious widow of Mao, Jiang Qing. Mao Zedong first gave a detailed account of his life to the American journalist, Edgar Snow, who was the first foreign newspaperman to talk to Mao. In his book *Red Star Over China* Snow gave a unique description of his many conversations with Mao and other Communist leaders in one of their strongholds in the north, Baoan. Snow's account of the autobiography which Mao told to him is still the basis for all others.

Mao Zedong was born on 26 December 1893, the eldest of four. Having started life as a poor peasant, Mao's father, tight-fisted and money-grubbing from his son's account, acquired four acres of land, so was reasonably well off by rural standards. The house where the Maos lived is spacious and solid, surrounded by trees. The village of Shaoshan, where the family lived, is in Hunan Province in the centre of China, neither one of the richest nor one of the poorest regions. It is famous for its fiery food and its hot-headed revolutionaries, and Mao Zedong was a true son of the soil.

From Mao's own account, his relationship with his father was hostile. Caught between an authoritarian teacher at his primary school and an authoritarian father, Mao rebelled early. The first revolt was at the age of ten. Threatened by a beating at school, he stayed away, then ran away from home for fear of a beating from his father. After three days of wandering in circles he returned home, and was surprised to be greeted by a mild reaction from both his teacher and his father. Even at that age he realised that his first protest had been effective. At thirteen, he threatened to drown himself in the village pond unless his father promised never to beat him again. No parent would relish his son drowning himself during a family quarrel, but in China the prospect of an eldest son committing suicide, so disqualifying himself from eventually performing the ancestral rites for his father and other forebears, was too appalling to contemplate. Mao's father apologised. Mao said 'I learned that when I defended my rights by open rebellion my father relented, but when I remained meek and submissive, he only beat me more.' Increasingly, he, his two brothers, his sister and even his gentle mother began to band together against his tyrannical father. This early realisation that rebellion paid off sowed the seeds for many of Mao's actions in later life.

At the age of sixteen Mao enrolled in a local primary school which taught 'Western learning'. Older, taller and scruffier than the other boys, he was apparently scoffed at, but made no attempt to become friends with them. But school was a haven for him, as it gave him the chance to read. And not only the Chinese classics which were part of the school syllabus, but also a miscellany of books about reformers and conquerors as diverse as Lincoln and Napoleon. At eighteen he enrolled in a secondary school in the provincial capital of Changsha, and there he again met with hostility and ostracism. Even at that age Mao seemed to be preparing himself for the decades ahead, when it often seemed as though the whole world was against him, and the world frequently included the other leaders of the Chinese Communist Party. Already he thrived on confrontation and self-sufficiency and was quite contemptuous of other people's opinions.

For the next few years Mao tried a variety of educational establishments, generally finding them circumscribed in curriculum and breadth of ideas. He enrolled in a bewildering range of colleges, from police to soap-making and, increasingly disillusioned, finally spent six solid months reading in the Hunan Provincial Library. His reading list was self-devised and eclectic. He read Adam Smith, John Stuart Mill, Darwin and Huxley, European and American history, Greek mythology, romances, poetry and every newspaper which he could lay his hands on. Mao always spent a disproportionate amount of his meagre allowance on books and papers. But one interesting sidelight on this future champion of the manual labourer is his admission that at that time, poor as he was, he used to buy water from the water-carriers because 'I, being a student, could not condescend to carrying'.

Eventually this man, who decades later was to be described as the Great Helmsman and Great Teacher of his people, decided that his vocation was to teach. At the First Normal College (a teachers' training college) Mao hated the compulsory courses, but met a man who was to have a great effect on his life – his Professor of Ethics, Yang Changji. Mao greatly admired the man and his teachings.

During his vacations Mao went off with friends on hikes through Hunan. They not only espoused the simplicity of peasant life, but also wanted to harden themselves physically by exposing themselves to inclement weather. In this Mao was much encouraged by Professor Yang, who had spent time in Britain, and not only admired the 'democratic life' of the British, as he put it, but also the strange British enthusiasm for such austerities as cold baths and brisk walks. So the young Mao did the same, and with each victory over a hostile environment came to believe firmly that man could always triumph over even the most inimical world. In the years to come, both the toughness of his body and the resilience of his mind were to stand him in good stead.

When Mao graduated from teachers' training college in 1918, many young Chinese were going abroad to study, and initially Mao was amongst those bound for France. But at the last moment he decided not to go, arguing that he did not yet know enough about his own country. It is hard to know whether this was the real reason. He may have realised that he lacked the ability to learn foreign languages, or believed that he might encounter even greater hostility outside his own country. But Mao also had a strong streak of chauvinism, and even at that early stage may have felt that China's destiny had to be forged from within China itself, and that foreign ideas could be partially, but not wholly, transplanted. We know that around this time he had already read the *Communist Manifesto* for the first time, as well as Kautsky's *Class Struggle*. Later he was to say that they had 'built in me a faith in Marxism'. However, there has always been some doubt as to whether he ever fully understood the Marxist classics.

Meanwhile Mao's admired Professor of Ethics, Yang Changji, had moved to Peking, and was teaching at Peking National University. He helped Mao to get a job as an assistant librarian at the university. But it was there that Mao's already nascent suspicion of intellectuals (ironic in a man who read voraciously and loved the world of ideas) was converted into a lifelong dislike and contempt. For the scholars who borrowed books would not condescend to talk to a mere assistant librarian. After 1949 China's intellectuals were to pay a collective price for the humiliation which some of their number had meted out to the young Mao, as they were sent to the countryside to do manual labour during the many political campaigns which followed the Communist victory.

But not everything was gloom and humiliation. Not only did Mao meet many of the men who were to become leaders of the Chinese Communist Party, but he also fell in love with and married Professor Yang's daughter, Yang Kaihui. Mao had been betrothed by his parents at the age of fourteen, but had never lived with the girl. Yang Kaihui was a true revolution-ary and soul-mate for Mao. Although they were often separ-ated whilst Mao was ranging the country organising Party activities and peasant insurrections, it appears to have been a compatible marriage, brought to a tragic end when Yang was publicly executed. Mao has often been blamed for having left Yang in Changsha at a time when his own activities were well known to the KMT, and when anyone associated with him was also under suspicion.

It is worth noting that six members of Mao's family were sacrificed to the revolution and the country. His middle brother was killed in the fighting in southern China, and his youngest in the north-west; his sister was executed in Hunan; he lost a nephew during the fighting in the Central Plain; during the Long March two of his children by his next wife, He Zizhen, were handed over to peasants to be looked after, and were never seen again. This second wife was also badly injured by shrapnel in a bombing attack. And a son of Mao's was killed during the Korean War. A high toll, but no higher than that suffered by many families during those decades.

He Zizhen was with Mao in the northern town of Yanan, where the Red Army settled in 1935 at the end of the Long March, and it was there that she and Mao divorced. There has always been some controversy over whether Mao and He were already divorced when Mao's third and last wife caught his eye in Yanan. Some say that Jiang Qing (or Lan Ping, as she was then known), a Shanghai actress, stole Mao away from He, but there is good evidence that He had already asked for a divorce on the grounds that Mao's affections had been alienated by another Shanghai actress, the ravishing Lily Wu. For all the revolutionary fervour of the Communist Party headquarters in Yanan, it was also fraught with affairs, scandals, divorce and the hectic relationships which seem to blossom in wartime. Many actresses, film stars and other exotic creatures, attracted by the lure of the left wing and because of the increasing lawlessness of cities like Shanghai, gravitated to Yanan, and there is no doubt that many of the Communist leaders found them irresistible compared with their own doughty, revolutionary wives.

Despite all the claims of revolutionary equality, what was sauce for the gander in Yanan was definitely not sauce for the goose. More than one wife of a Communist leader asked for a divorce, only to be told that in the interests of the revolution she must stick by her husband. Then a short time afterwards the same husband's eye was caught by an attractive new-comer, and suddenly the rules were changed and the man was granted a divorce.

Whatever the circumstances of Mao's divorce from He Zizhen, Jiang Qing certainly became pregnant by Mao, and later married him, with the very reluctant consent of the leadership, and on condition that Mao kept her out of politics. And until the 1960s Mao did manage to keep his slim, vital and ambitious wife out of mainstream politics.

Throughout his life Mao Zedong deliberately acted out the role of peasant leader. Whilst part of the characterisation was, no doubt, perfectly natural, it also seems only too likely that Mao took an almost perverse pleasure in his self-assigned part. Visitors to Yanan described how he used to search himself for fleas; his complete indifference to both his appear-ance and even his cleanliness was legendary. His long hair used to fall over his face as he read. His language was earthy and to the point. But coupled with the barnyard image was another, more complex Mao. Many who met him spoke of his remoteness, his obvious intellectualism and even a quality of effeminacy which was described as faintly repellant.

Zhou Enlai was a totally different personality. He came from a traditional Confucian family, and despite his enor-mous popular appeal he always retained a patrician image. His family members had been scholars and mandarins for generations, living in the rich and developed eastern provinces of Zhejiang and Jiangsu. Zhou Enlai was educated at a Westernised university and, unlike Mao, was one of those young Chinese who went to France on a work-study pro-gramme. Zhou was a founder member of the French branch of the Chinese Communist Party and whilst in France he organised protests against the government in China, gained a thorough knowledge of French factory conditions and the situation of the French proletariat, and made frequent visits to Berlin on Party business. When he returned to China he helped to organise the April 1927 uprising in Shanghai, and barely escaped with his life in the KMT massacre of the Communists.

Until 1935 Mao Zedong and Zhou Enlai were frequently on opposite sides of the ideological fence. One particular area of disagreement was over the treatment of the rich peasants. As a more orthodox Marxist, Zhou took a Stalinist view of the matter and believed in a harsh approach. But the wily Mao felt that to confiscate their property at that stage of the revolution would simply alienate them, at a time when the Communist movement could ill afford such alienation. They could be dealt with later. Zhou accused him of capitulating to the rich peasants, and in addition accused Mao of militarism, pragmatism, opportunism and 'general ideological poverty'. Harsh words. By 1933 Zhou had edged Mao out of leading military and political roles. But in 1935, at a crucial meeting that was to establish Mao's leadership role for the next forty years, Zhou accepted Mao's line and over the next four decades, until the death of both men in 1976, was his loyal right-hand man. Some would argue that he was too loyal, and could have done more to dilute Mao's increasingly extreme policies.

One always hears the most extravagant praise of Zhou Enlai. He had extraordinary charm and presence and great powers of persuasion, which was why he was given the unenviable task of acting as the Communist Party's liaison man with the KMT in the city of Chongqing (Chungking) after the KMT had moved its government there following the start of the Anti-Japanese War in 1937. Zhou the suave diplomat acted as go-between in the uneasy United Front between the two sides, and needed all his reserves of patience and stamina during those treacherous years.

Not only was Zhou Enlai the antithesis of Mao in character, but also in appearance. Of medium height and slim build, he was always immaculate. It was said that his beautifully cut suits, with their high-collared Sun Yat-sen jackets, were made to measure by an old Shanghai tailor, and they certainly looked as though they were. When I was working in Peking in the early and mid-1970s I saw Zhou on several occasions, and although he was by then elderly and very ill he still exuded charm and personality, and had an amused and quizzical smile. His gestures were very controlled, as though he did not want to waste an ounce of energy. Although we did not know it at the time, he already knew that he was dying of cancer. Zhou Enlai's popular image is perhaps best summed up by a Chinese joke about a row which he had with the Soviet leader Krushchev at a time of growing Sino-Soviet animosity. The bluff Krushchev, enraged by Zhou's urbane refusal to let him have his own way, is said to have compared his own peasant background with Zhou's more bourgeois origins. 'How could we possibly have anything in common?' stormed Krushchev. Unruffled, so the story goes, Zhou replied, 'Mr Krushchev, we have at least one thing in common. We have both betrayed our class origins.'

The backgrounds of other leaders will be decribed later in the book, as they begin to play a more public role, but another leading Communist who deserves mention early on is Lin Biao, who was to assume a position of great importance. During the early years of the Civil and Anti-Japanese Wars his brilliance as a military tactician was of crucial importance to the war effort. He was born in 1908 in central China, the son of an unsuccessful factory owner. The young Lin studied at the Whampoa Military Academy, where, ironically, Chiang Kai-shek was Commandant at the time. At the age of twenty he was a colonel in the elite Fourth KMT Army, but in August 1927, following the coup against the left wing of the KMT, he decamped with his troops to join the Communists. Astonishingly, he was never wounded, despite having engaged in at least one hundred front-line battles, and having a huge price on his head. By the age of thirty this small, nondescript man's reputation as a formidable military tactician was known even outside China.

After the 1927 massacre of the Shanghai Communists the Party changed its tactics. It organised a series of abortive peasant uprisings, with disastrous loss of life. Stalin urged simultaneous popular proletarian uprisings in the mistaken belief that the Chinese proletariat was ripe for revolution, which it was not. Meanwhile Mao, ever the opportunist, was marshalling whatever support he could. He did not hesitate to exploit family and clan groupings, secret societies, and other traditional forces which could act as a springboard for the new social order which he believed would eventually emerge.

Young students who had received political training in the cities now returned to their native areas and used old family ties to start their work of radicalising the peasantry.

Four out of five people worked in the agricultural sector (and only recently has that ratio changed), but the distribution of land led to extreme poverty. Some 10 per cent of the population owned about 70 per cent of the land. Rents levied by the landlords were often extortionate, sometimes as high as 70 per cent of the crop, with no remission in times of bad harvests. When local warlords needed funds for their armies they levied extra taxes, often many years in advance. The early 1930s were a bad time for China's peasants. Economic recession, coupled with appalling weather in the early part of the decade, made life intolerable. Troops requisitioned what food there was, and there was a heavy burden of direct and indirect taxes. There was terrible famine in certain provinces. In Henan, corpses littered the countryside, their bellies swollen with the bark, grass and roots which were their last resort.

As always in time of famine, the peasants migrated to the cities and swelled the huge numbers of urban beggars. Childen with stick-like limbs and swollen bellies begged on the streets and in the restaurants, waiting for people to finish eating so that they could snatch the scraps. Deformed, often retarded, these people made up a veritable army of beggars. Parents frequently sold their children, the boys to become servants and labourers, and the girls to beome concubines, prostitutes or dance-hall girls.

The country was ripe for revolution, but the peasants were not willing to rush headlong into an uncertain future. In China, the richest landlord in the village and the poorest tenant were frequently related through family ties, however tenuous, and a rebellion against the landlord was a rebellion against one's own clan. Furthermore, if the land of the rich were confiscated, and the Communists were then to leave the area which they had 'liberated', how could the peasants be sure that there would not be terrible reprisals by those whose land had been taken away? It was only in those regions where the Communist Red Army was seen to have some degree of permanency that the peasants were willing to throw away their fears and their conservatism, and to involve themselves firstly in practical questions of taxation and grain distribution and then in the highly political area of 'class struggle'.

The role of the peasants in the Communist Revolution was the source of the most fundamental disagreement that Mao Zedong was to have with those of his fellow Communists who had been trained in Moscow, or who otherwise had a more orthodox view of Marxism and Leninism. To them the only correct view was that the revolution would be based on the urban proletariat, as had happened in Russia. They viewed the peasants with suspicion, regarding them as conservative and politically backward, which was quite true at the time. Mao, who had by then developed his own brand of Marxism, believed that in a country in which 80 per cent of the population lived in the rural areas, it was unrealistic to envisage a revolution based on the cities. Mao knew that the peasants were politically illiterate, but believed that the miserable conditions under which they lived could be used to heighten their political awareness. And Mao turned out to be right.

Before the formation of the Chinese Red Army, China had only known conscript armies – badly paid and badly treated by their officers. But as early as 1930 peasants were voluntarily joining the Communist forces, and were even becoming officers, almost unheard of in a Chinese army. By the spring of 1934 nearly 70 per cent of the Communist First Front Army were peasants. But the disadvantage of the majority of these recruits was their illiteracy. Until China's current leader, Deng Xiaoping, started to reform the Chinese People's Liberation Army (PLA) in the 1980s, the lack of an educated officer class was a major problem. And these same officers had a lingering peasant mistrust of a modern, professional approach to military affairs.

The Communist Red Army was like no other in China's history. Traditionally, Chinese soldiers did not enjoy a glowing reputation. There was an old saying that one does not use good iron to make nails, nor good men to make soldiers. The conscript armies were frequently marauding, brutalised hordes, who looted, raped and pillaged. But the Red Army transformed this traditional image, and until its brutal suppression of the mass demonstrations in Tiananmen Square in early June 1989, the Army's image was untarnished in the eyes of the Chinese people.

Gradually the battered and suspicious population realised that the Communist leaders meant it when they said that their troops paid for everything that they needed, did not molest women, and did not leave destruction in their wake. They were famous for their rules of conduct, known as the Three Main Rules of Discipline and the Eight Points for Attention (the Chinese have a positive mania for attaching numbers to every campaign and undertaking). And what these slogans boiled down to was the simple assertion that this was a professional army which did as it would be done by. If they borrowed a needle and thread they returned it. If they removed a door to use as a plank bed for the night (a common occurrence), they replaced it. They did not even accept food as a gift, but insisted on paying for it. They helped with domestic and farming chores. This was not completely altruistic. On the contrary, it was the best form of propaganda for the Communist movement. The propaganda teams travelled the rural areas teaching the peasants revolutionary songs and acting out plays which not only added colour to the peasants' barren lives, but also contained the pill of revolution tucked into the sweets of entertainment.

This unique army had great appeal, and in the areas through which it passed there was no shortage of volunteers. Many of the recruits were very young, not even in their teens. Known as Little Red Devils, they ran errands, did chores and eventually became formidable fighters. Political training was as rigorous as military, and the soldiers had no doubts about what they were fighting for. Soldiers committees ensured democracy, and officers and men all got the same low pay.

By the spring of 1934 the KMT troops, with much better weaponry and tanks, were pressing hard on the Communist bases in the southern Province of Jiangxi. Since the situation in the south had clearly become too dangerous for the Communist forces, Mao decided to break out of the KMT encirclement and move north with the other Communist forces from adjacent areas. He planned that they would then engage the Japanese troops which had already occupied Manchuria and Shanghai, although the war against the Japanese did not begin in earnest until 1937. This move from south to north was known as the Long March, and was one of the greatest epic tales of all time.

Burdened as they were with women and children, printing presses, factory lathes, sewing machines, silver bullion and a mass of other equipment which they needed to be self-sufficient, they were unwieldy and vulnerable. By the time they had broken clear of the KMT encirclement they had suffered as many as 30 000 casualties and lost much of their baggage train.

Over the next year Mao's views on military tactics were to be honed to a fine point. His enemies accused him of 'flightism' because he would avoid battle whenever possible. Mao was no coward, but he believed that it was a waste of his men to engage in a battle unless he was sure that they would win. Mao was a worthy student of the great Chinese strategist of ancient times, Sun Zi, who was one of the earliest proponents of guerrilla tactics. Mao believed that one only fought if one had to; that it was perfectly reasonable to retreat in the face of superior firepower; that one used surprise and deceit wherever possible to defeat the enemy; that one equipped one's own troops with weaponry captured from the enemy.

In those early months of the Long March, Mao had to employ every guerrilla tactic to shake off the harassing KMT troops. The Communist forces had to strike out to the west through appallingly inhospitable terrain, where the enemy were fewer in number. The region is extremely mountainous, and these are not gentle mountains but precipitous drops, a dreadful challenge to a tired, underfed, overburdened army. Many fell to their deaths, froze, died of illness or drowned in the fast-flowing rivers. To avoid the pursuing enemy the troops had to make innumerable detours, often retracing their steps. They travelled by night to avoid detection. They were forced to cross a notorious swamp in the western Province of Qinghai, and many were sucked into the ooze. They were frequently attacked by hostile tribes of minority peoples, who had so often been attacked by Han Chinese armies (the Hans form the overwhelming majority of the population) that they had no reason to suppose that this particular army had anything different in mind. There was never enough food, and the grasses and roots which the troops ate gave them constant diarrhoea. The wounded and sick, which frequently included the Chinese leaders, had to be carried up steep mountain paths.

Not only were there natural disasters and harrying enemy troops to battle against, but in the early months of the Long March the leaders were in constant conflict with each other over both military and political tactics. But in January 1935, at the south-western town of Zunyi, the Communist leadership held a watershed meeting. And now Mao was to avenge himself for all the epithets that had been flung at him, for it was clear that, at least militarily, he had been right. Now his orthodox opponents were forced to eat crow, but the wily Zhou Enlai, sensing that the tide had turned, changed sides. Mao was now both military and *de facto* political leader of the Chinese Communist Party. But even more to the point, it was the first time that the leader of the Chinese Communist movement had been chosen without the imprimatur of Moscow. The Russians were not pleased.

One year and some 6000 miles after breaking out of their southern base, the various forces which made up the Red Army straggled into Yanan, in the northern Province of Shaanxi. This mountain fastness was to remain their base for the next decade. Here the troops were able to recruit their forces for the battles ahead. They were a painfully diminished army. Of the 300 000 or so troops which had made up the entire Red Army, only about 30 000 had survived the rigours of the Long March and the warfare along its route.

Yanan is a well protected place. Surrounded by mountains, it is built on the soil known as loess. This soft, friable, yellow earth lends itself to the hollowing out of caves in which many of the population still live. And it was in these caves, warm in winter and cool in summer, that the Communist leaders and their men were to pass a troglodyte existence. I visited Yanan in 1973, and even then it was apparent that an enemy would have a hard task to penetrate it. Shortly after I arrived it started to rain, and the visibility was so poor that for three days the plane could not take off. Furthermore, the heavy rain had washed the road away. If the place was inaccessible in 1973, one can imagine what it was like in the 1930s. Even in 1973 Yanan was still desperately poor. People ate little besides noodles and steamed bread. The general standard of living was very low. The people of Yanan must have questioned the benefits of the revolution which had been launched from their small town four decades earlier.

Having temporarily escaped one enemy, the KMT, the

Communists, and indeed the whole of China, now faced another, formidable foe – the Japanese. They had already taken control of China's major industrial base, Manchuria, in 1931, and of that other vital economic base, Shanghai, the following year. It was clear that they were not going to stop there. Already, on the Long March, Mao Zedong had opened up negotiations with all sectors of the Chinese nation that might prove to be useful allies against Japan. These included minority nationalities, secret societies and other groups which might not normally have been considered ideal allies. Chiang Kai-shek's policy of appeasement had already allowed the Japanese to consolidate their position in China, and Mao knew that the Nationalists and the Communists would have to sink their differences and unite against the common enemy. Chiang viewed such an alliance with considerable distaste, but one of Chiang's own marshals agreed with the Communist position, and in the so-called 'Xi'an Incident' of 1936 conspired with the Communists to kidnap Chiang and force him to agree on a United Front. But it was far from united. It was well known that Chiang blocked supplies of weapons and other goods to the Communists in the north, determined that they should not get the chance to build up their supplies for any future use against his own troops. The Communists and the Nationalists accused each other of not launching sufficiently determined attacks against the Japanese, and it is true that Mao only risked his troops when there was a good chance of inflicting heavy damage on the enemy. But his guerrillas harassed the Japanese constantly, and it was not difficult to mobilise the local peasantry against the Japanese in those areas through which the enemy had passed.

The Anti-Japanese War started in earnest in 1937 after a minor incident in which Chinese and Japanese troops clashed on the outskirts of Peking. By the end of July the Japanese had taken Peking and Tianjin (Tientsin), and by the autumn of the following year were in control of all the major cities down to the Yangtse River, including Nanjing (Nanking), Shanghai and Wuhan. Much has been written about the horrors of the war, and the appalling cruelty which the Japanese meted out to the Chinese living in the cities and villages which they overran. The most notorious event was the conquest of Nanjing, where it is estimated that at least 200 000 Chinese were savagely killed within several days. This was approximately one-fifth of the population of the city. It is believed that about 10 million Chinese died during the course of the war, and the scars left on China affect Sino-Japanese relations to the present day.

Chiang Kai-shek's capital had been based in Nanjing since 1934. In 1938 it moved first to Hankou (Hankow), then to Chongqing (Chungking), where it was to stay for the duration of the war. It is a city with an appalling climate – cold and damp in winter, hot and humid in the summer, and misty the whole year round. But it is strategically perfect. Situated as it is in the mountains of the south-west, when the United States joined in the war its remoteness enabled the Americans to fly in supplies for the KMT government from Burma. The officials of the KMT government lived, not in luxury, but in a much greater degree of comfort than the rest of the population. The war was taking a terrible toll, and there were beggars and refugees everywhere. Disease and malnutrition were facts of life. To add to the misery, the city was subjected to constant bombing raids by the Japanese.

Bedraggled, exhausted and demoralised KMT troops were to be seen on all the roads in the south. They were no match for the better equipped and better disciplined Japanese troops. One old KMT soldier told me that his troop was so resentful of being bullied by their officers and having food and pay withheld that they finally mutinied and went over to the Communists. It was said that Chiang was saving his troops for 'the real enemy', the Communists, of which he said 'The Japanese are like a disease of the skin, but the Communists are like a disease of the heart.' Chiang had good reason to be apprehensive, for the Communist bases were gradually spreading over an ever-larger area of north China, in preparation for the day when the Japanese would have gone, and then the true enemy would have to be vanquished.

In the meantime the Red Army was suffering great hardship in Yanan, as Chiang Kai-shek's troops had blockaded them once again. They were short of everything, including food and clothes. But throughout the Yanan base area the peasants saw that the soldiers suffered as much as they did, and this did much to win over the local population. The creeping influence of the Red Army continued. Fighting as little as possible, they gradually moved down through the Japanese defences, and by the time the Second World War ended in 1945 the Communists controlled a great swathe of northern China, with some 90 million people within their sphere of influence.

Now the battle lines were drawn for the final struggle. Both the KMT and the Communist troops were exhausted after years of war, shortage of basic necessities and war material. But the KMT were much better off, for they had the support of the Americans, who supplied them with equipment to defeat the Communist menace. Although many State Department people with a thorough knowledge of China had advised the American government that Chiang Kai-shek's KMT was not the best choice for the future government of China, the fear of Communism sweeping Asia was a potent factor in the American decision to back Chiang. However, even in Chiang's stronghold in Chongqing there was a growing feeling that China's future lay with the Communists. It was well known that morale in the Communist areas was extremely high, despite the miserable material conditions, whilst in the south there was growing disillusionment with the corrupt KMT. There was increasing poverty and disorder, and Chiang made a fatal mistake. He branded as traitors people in cities which had been under Japanese occupation, and so alienated a great percentage of the population whose support he desperately needed in the final battle against the Communists.

Meanwhile Stalin had sent Soviet advisers to help the fledgling Chinese Communist Party, and to instal as leaders of the CCP Chinese who had either been trained in Moscow, or who had an orthodox view of Marxism and Leninism. But Mao himself had generally been in contention with these Moscow-approved leaders. Stalin was not pleased with Mao's emergence as Party leader, and viewed with apprehension the possible emergence of a powerful Communist state right on the borders of the Soviet Union. Stalin made it clear that he wanted Chiang and the KMT as the future leaders of China. With the defeat of the Japanese in 1945 the Russians moved into Manchuria and secured various concessions from the Chinese government, such as as control of the railway. When the Russian troops finally withdrew from Manchuria they took with them industrial plant and equipment as 'war booty' – plant which was desperately needed by the Chinese.

Although the Communists were in control of the north when the Japanese were defeated, the Russians agreed to the clause in the Yalta Agreement which stated that the Japanese should surrender to the KMT and not the Communists. The Americans flew Chiang and KMT troops to the north to accept the surrender of the Japanese, and also transported over 500000 Nationalist troops to north China to prevent the Communists from moving south. But from the point of view of the Chinese Communists, the ultimate Soviet betrayal was their proposal, when it was clear that the Communists were going to win the Civil War, that China should be partitioned. Stalin covertly proposed that Chiang and the KMT should rule south of the Yangtse River, and Mao and the Communists north of the Yangtse. Thus Stalin would have a weak and divided China on his southern border. Mao was not impressed.

Following the defeat of the Japanese, the KMT and the Communists were engaged in a final, four-year battle for supremacy, and the population suffered once again. Millions of refugees streamed all over the countryside and into the beleaguered cities. There was not enough food. Industry was in chaos. Inflation was so bad that people needed a wheelbarrow full of notes to buy a few groceries. Friends who were teaching in Nanjing at the time told me that the moment they were paid they dashed out to convert their pay into silver dollars, as it would have halved in value by the afternoon. Corruption was rife. The KMT had police spies everywhere, ready to arrest and execute anyone suspected of having Communist sympathies. In many provinces there was terrible poverty, with opium addiction the only release. Bandits roamed the countryside and robbed trains and road vehicles with impunity. Cautious travellers moved in groups for added protection. The country was desperate for a solution.

The Communist troops were bombed out of Yanan in 1947, and they endured terrible hardship in their efforts to avoid the Nationalists. Within a month even the frugal food which they had eaten in Yanan had been reduced to a revolting porridge of 'flour and elm seeds'. They travelled at night, carrying the sick and wounded, hampered even further by the slow-moving cattle which they were reluctant to abandon. At one stage Mao Zedong and Zhou Enlai were both so weak that they had to be carried on stretchers. But the Communists continued their hit-and-run tactics, drawing 400 000 KMT troops into a position in which they were cut off and neutralised. By the end of 1947 Chiang Kai-shek had lost Manchuria, the Communists had a vital industrial base under their control, and they were set for the all-important assault on the Central China Plain. The campaign lasted over two months, Chiang lost another half a million of his best men, and his army was emasculated. Not only did the Communists fight an excellent tactical war, but their troops were still bursting with morale, whereas many of the KMT troops were thoroughly demoralised. Peking surrendered peacefully, and the Communists found themselves on the banks of the great river that cuts the country in two from west to east − the Yangtse.

From then on matters moved with extraordinary speed, and the People's Liberation Army pushed along the river to take Chiang's current capital at Nanjing. By October 1949 the Communist troops had reached Canton and Chiang Kai-shek and the Nationalists had fled to the island of Taiwan. The Communists were themselves amazed at the speed of their victory. The more cautious had thought that they might have to endure another two decades of civil war before the final victory, and even the ever-optimistic Mao Zedong had not expected a total victory before the beginning of the 1950s.

Yet here he now was, standing on the Gate of Heavenly Peace, surveying his exhausted, cheering people. But what had he inherited? China had been almost destroyed by decades of war. The industrial base, never very strong, was in ruins. There was poverty, malnutrition and endemic disease on an apocalyptic scale. The country still crawled with bandits, KMT symathisers, crooks and rogues in their millions. The big cities teemed with beggars, prostitutes and the dispossessed. China had only one real ally, and a somewhat untrustworthy one at that − the Soviet Union. Mao Zedong and his fellow Communists were, to all intents and purposes, on their own. Only a man of Mao's arrogance, optimism, vision and determination could have contemplated with equanimity the task of raising his people from the dust.

CHAPTER TWO

A
FRAGILE
UNITY

Harsher critics of Mao Zedong might argue that he spent two decades helping the Chinese people to 'stand up', as he himself put it, and the next two decades bringing them once again to their knees. But the period from 1949 to 1956 is now looked back on as a Golden Age, and it is worth asking why. Against all the odds the Communists had won China, and at a speed which surprised even themselves. They were masters of the most populous country on earth, but now they had to rule it. The Chinese have a saying that 'You can conquer a country on horseback, but you cannot rule it on horseback', and the new leaders were only too aware that they might have millions of enthusiastic followers, but for the most part they were illiterate peasants who did not have the slightest idea how to manage anything except their own plots of land.

Not only was the new Communist government short of expertise, but the areas in which they needed it were the cities of the centre and south of the country, over which the Communist forces had had little influence during the previous two decades of war. Their base areas had been largely in the north and the north-east, and not only were there many in the south of the country who were deeply suspicious of the Communists, but there were still large numbers of KMT sympathisers and supporters around. Mao Zedong and his fellow leaders knew that in order to unite the whole of their disparate country they had to develop the economy as swiftly as possible. This meant that for the time being at least, they needed the co-operation of the factory owners and people of 'dubious' class-background. So although time was running

out for the 'capitalists', they were allowed to go on managing
their factories.

Even Mao Zedong, that arch-supporter of the Chinese
peasantry, acknowledged that the time for the countryside to
lead the cities was over, and the time for the cities to lead the
countryside had begun – an orthodox Marxist-Leninist view.
Echoing Stalin, he also believed that China had to give
priority to industrialisation. As far as we know, there was no
doubt in the minds of any of the Chinese leaders that China
would have to follow the Soviet model. For all the irritations
in their relationship, the Soviet Union was still their closest
ally, and there was no better socialist model available. But the
borrowing was not an unquestioning one, and as the Chinese
leaders became more confident they also became more aware
of what would suit their country and what would not. They
knew that without a sound agricultural base there could be no
steady industrial development. They knew the difficulties
which the USSR had encountered in agricultural development, and wanted to avoid making the same mistakes.

In 1950 the Communist leaders adopted a gradual
approach to development. Although they were tightening
their grip on the private sector, their plan was not to
antagonise the people whose help they needed. Civil servants
were kept on in their posts, and factory managers helped to
revive factory production. Not surprisingly, there were still
considerable tensions as Communist Party cadres were gradually moved into the factories to assume a leading role
although they lacked experience in production techniques.
Generally, these cadres backed the workers in any dispute
with management, and this often led to disruption of output.

At the same time as the new Chinese leadership was
tackling its economic problems, it was also making vigorous
efforts to wipe out the evils of the old society. Prostitutes were
rounded up and 're-educated', taught a trade and put into
useful employment. The jobless and the beggars were put to
work to repair the damage of years of war. Cities had to be
rebuilt, people had to be organised in gainful employment, the
educational system re-established, a public health system
initiated, and it all required a great and sustained enthusiasm.
Visitors to China during those early years of the People's
Republic spoke with admiration of the steady elimination of

beggars, venereal disease, crime, inflation and hopelessness. They also noted, but with disapproval, the authorised vandalism in Peking. The massive city walls were ripped down, along with the graceful arches along many of the main roads. This was allegedly to make way for the streams of traffic which would eventually flow through Peking, but was also a most effective way of doing away with landmarks of the imperial past. Luckily, the destruction stopped short of the Temple of Heaven, the Imperial Palace, and a few other architectural wonders. It was said that Zhou Enlai personally ordered the destruction.

As if China were not already sufficiently burdened with trying to revive a country which had been shattered by years of war, its problems were exacerbated by the Korean War, which erupted in 1950. There was much debate amongst the leadership as to whether China should join in, and after two or three days of agonising Mao decided that it should. The losses which China suffered were appalling, as this time they were fighting against sophisticated weaponry, and well trained and motivated opponents. The cost was not only immense in human terms, but also in economic, for China had to pay the Soviet Union for all the weapons which it supplied to the Chinese, and the able-bodied men who should have been helping to restore China's economy were fighting someone else's war. But there was an important plus side, for the Chinese gained enormously in regional prestige, and showed the international community that they were a force to be reckoned with.

However, this foreign adventure meant that economic planning continued to be done on a year-to-year basis, and although nationwide planning began in 1953, it was not until 1955 that the First Five Year Plan of 1953–57 was actually ratified. Although it was originally envisaged that the private sector would only be very gradually linked to the public sector, by 1952 some 70 to 80 per cent of heavy industry and about 40 per cent of light industry was already owned by the state.

The social and economic successes of those early years of the Chinese People's Republic were considerable, and those sectors of the population which had most to gain worked enthusiastically for the new order. Today, many Chinese look back on that period as one in which the entire country pulled together, and they maintain that there was a selfless fervour which was never to be found again. That may be a slight exaggeration, but there was certainly a good deal of truth in it. But the darker side of the Golden Age were the harsh campaigns which had taken place almost from the beginning of the new era.

Dark side

Any fears which the 'national bourgeoisie' had felt about their future under a Communist regime had by 1953 been amply justified with two extremely harsh mass campaigns. Quite apart from a campaign to root out 'counter-revolutionaries' (facilitated by the tensions caused by the Korean War), there were also the so-called Three-Antis and the Five-Antis campaigns of 1951 and 1952. The former was aimed at corrupt cadres, and the latter at the national bourgeoisie. There was considerable large-scale violence, with mass trials, especially of those accused of being counter-revolutionaries. These were attended by tens of thousands of people and engendered a climate of fear and repression. As many as half a million people are believed to have cracked under the pressure and committed suicide. There is no doubt that there were still many KMT spies around, and KMT sympathisers committed acts of sabotage, but the term 'counter-revolutionary' has always been loosely defined in China, and has frequently been applied to people who merely question the absolute authority of the Chinese Communist Party. What the Five-Antis campaign was really attacking was the entire set of urban values which did not conform to Marxist–Leninist orthodoxy. Capitalists were accused of real or imaginary crimes, and had swingeing fines imposed on them. The only way to pay was by selling large amounts of their stock to the state, thus strengthening state control over enterprises.

It was at this time that Thought Reform once again became an important factor in political education. This had been applied to intellectuals in Yanan in the early 1940s, and continued to be a vital factor in the Chinese Communist Party's attempt to change the soul of Chinese man. The techniques used produced truly devastating results. A small group would study a policy document or article together, and then discuss what it meant. One could not opt out by saying nothing. Passivity was not allowed. Everyone had to give an opinion, which was then criticised by others in the group. Innermost thoughts were exposed to be poked at and dissected. The participants had to write self-confessions, declaring that their previous thinking had been deviant or bourgeois. The first confession was never accepted, and the victim usually had to write several, each one baring another layer of his soul. What was required was a complete surrender, followed by catharsis, as a phoenix arose from its old ideological ashes. That was the theory, and in many cases it was highly successful, but for thousands of people the psychological and emotional trauma was so great that they were mentally destroyed and committed suicide. China lost many of its great intellectuals this way. Either they were physically dead, or so cowed that they might as well have been.

Meanwhile, the most important question for Mao Zedong and his colleagues was the path of China's transformation into a socialist state. It was accepted, for the time being at least, that the Soviet model required a large capital input into heavy industry, and agricultural production had to be boosted to provide the necessary capital. So the major question was – how was China to achieve a considerably greater agricultural output?

Obviously the peasants had to be motivated to produce more, and the agricultural sector had to be so ordered as to achieve the maximum output. The answer was land reform. This had already been carried out in North-East China, where the Communists had been in control during the 1940s. Peasants were grouped into Mutual Aid Teams (MATs), in which they pooled their tools, animals and labour resources. This had not been too difficult to achieve, as Chinese peasants had traditionally joined together in groups at harvest time to help each other reap, thresh and store the grain as quickly as possible. But in the centre and south of the country even this basic transformation had to be achieved.

The eventual aim of the leadership was a complete redistribution of the land, and thus the destruction of a system of networks which had existed for centuries. In the villages some might be rich and some might be very poor, but often the majority were interrelated. The clan, the temple and even the secret society were all important factors in the web of village loyalties, and no one was going to risk breaking that binding web unless there was a degree of certainty that it would be replaced by something even more binding.

By the end of 1950, impatient with the pace of change, Mao and his colleagues introduced more radical policies. The whole process of land reform was to be speeded up, and class struggle was the weapon. All villagers were given a class identification. The property of the landlords was confiscated and distributed. So-called 'speak bitterness' meetings were held, at which the poor peasants were enouraged to talk about what they had suffered at the hands of the landlords. These meetings engendered great emotion and often led to violence in which the landlords were murdered. In addition to such spontaneous violence there were also public trials and executions, and years later Zhou Enlai said that some two million had been executed over the whole land reform period.

This stepping up of the pace of land reform was successful in that it broke the power of the old elite and distributed some 43 per cent of the land to about 60 per cent of the rural population. The peasants now had the courage to support the new order. It must be said that at this stage the rich peasants were not the target of land reform. Mao believed that he needed the co-operation of the innumerable rich peasants, many of whom were far from rich anyway, but were merely less poor than the poor. The Chinese had seen the systematic destruction of the rich peasant class in the Soviet Union and knew what a blow this had proved to agricultural output. They did not intend to make the same mistake. At least, not yet.

The Mutual Aid Teams were just the first step towards collectivisation, and the next was the organisation of peasants into co-operatives. These did not happen in significant numbers until 1952–53, and for the next three years collectivisation was subjected to a stop-go policy, whilst the Chinese leadership debated at length the speed at which they should move. The pragmatic economist, Chen Yun, believed that the peasants needed to be stimulated with material incentives. Once they had sold their produce the peasants would want to spend their extra income on consumer goods, so more money should be invested in light industry to produce such consumer goods. At the same time there should be increased capital input into heavy industry. Mao's own inclination was to rely on the peasant masses' revolutionary fervour to increase production.

In January 1956 a twelve-year draft programme was approved to boost agricultural output. Although there was emphasis on the importance of scientific and technical inputs and material incentives, the goals were still wildly ambitious, with projected increases in grain yields of up to 140 per cent. Another important development in 1956 was the holding in September of the Eighth Party Congress, the first for eleven years. There was an emphasis on the importance of steady advance, and both rash advance as well as 'right conservatism' were condemned. It was at that same meeting that Mao first proposed the creation of 'two fronts' within the leadership, and indicated that in the near future he would move into the 'second front'. This would then release him from day-to-day responsibility for the running of the country, and allow him to think about China's future in a broader sense. The post of Party Chairman was also created for Mao to take on when he eventually retired, for at that time Mao was State Chairman, and the equivalent Party post did not yet exist. A further interesting development was that Mao Zedong Thought, which had been enshrined as the guiding ideology of the CCP at the Seventh Party Congress in 1945 was deleted from the new Party Constitution. The political report to the congress was presented by Liu Shaoqi, which bolstered his status and indicated that he was in line to take over from Mao when the latter eventually retired.

Liu Shaoqi now began to play an increasingly important and public role as a leader of the CCP. Although he came from the same province as Mao, Hunan, he was a very different type of person, both physically and temperamentally. By now Mao was distinctly stocky in build, whilst Liu was very slender, with hair that was soon snow-white. There was nothing flamboyant about this Moscow-trained Party man. Where Mao's political experience had been mainly in the rural areas, Liu's had been in the 'white areas' in the cities, and so his political training was much more along traditional Soviet lines. He married the beautiful Wang Guangmei, who came from an undeniably bourgeois background. Liu did not support a rash pace of development, but a step-by-step advance. He believed in the supremacy of the Party rather than that of one individual. He and Mao were cut from very different templates, and it is interesting that Mao viewed Liu as a suitable successor.

By 1956 the leadership had agreed that the agricultural co-operatives were the tool with which to boost production, and that they also represented an important ideological advance. Where the leaders disagreed was over the pace at which the co-operative movement should advance. As far as one can tell, there was reasonably free debate about the steps forward, and those for or against a certain position spoke their minds without fear of stern reprisals. Against all the odds the economy was on a firmer footing and China was beginning to evolve its own model of development and rely less slavishly on the Soviet model. But soon there was to be an end to this degree of unity, and 1957 saw a change of pace and policy which would contribute to a split with the Soviet Union and begin to open fissures in the unity of the Chinese leadership that would eventually become gaping chasms.

Two traumas hit China in quick succession. One was the Hundred Flowers Movement, followed closely by the Anti-Rightist Campaign, and the other was the Great Leap Forward. In January 1956 at a major Party conference, Zhou Enlai proposed a number of ways to fan the Chinese intellectuals' enthusiasm for the revolution. He advocated that they should be given better pay and working conditions, be treated with more respect, and that their expertise should be fully utilised. Mao Zedong certainly endorsed these views, and in May of that year made his famous speech which included the call to 'let a hundred flowers bloom, let a hundred schools contend'. The 'hundred schools' referred to the so-called Hundred Schools of Thought of the late Zhou period (722 – 221 BC) – a nice classical touch. Intellectuals were encouraged to debate all areas except the political. They needed strong encouragement, as many were still feeling nervous as a result of the harsh treatment meted out to one of their number the previous year. The man in question, Hu Feng, had been openly critical of the Party, and as a result had been imprisoned and had suffered a nervous breakdown. With this lesson in mind, it was no wonder that other intellectuals were reluctant to speak their minds.

It has sometimes been argued that Mao knew that there was smouldering discontent amongst the intellectuals, and by calling on them to speak out was laying a trap to snare them all. He had always mistrusted and disliked intellectuals and suspected them of never quite having the best interests of the Party at heart. However, there is no documentation to support the idea, and it seems only too likely that Mao genuinely wanted to hear what they had to say, and had no idea that such a storm of criticism would be unleashed. For eventually the intellectuals did speak out. The scientists began to question the authority of Party officials to make scientific policy without having any idea of what they were talking about, and they demanded to be allowed to spend more time on scientific research and less on politics. Encouraged by this, the young writers began to criticise, and their criticisms were more specifically political. Leaders such as Mao and the cultural and ideological guru Zhou Yang appeared to encourage the debate. But by mid-May of 1957 things were getting out of hand. Students at Peking University started to put up Big Character Posters, as they were known, questioning the relevance of politics to intellectual work. They also demanded that the right to free speech should be enshrined in law. As criticism of individual officials turned into criticism of the whole system, it became apparent to Mao that the demon of Western liberalism, which he hoped had been swallowed up by Soviet intellectual theories, was still alive and well and extremely vociferous. On 8 June the tide turned.

Mao Zedong was shaken by the rash of criticism that erupted from the intellectuals. And yet it is interesting to ask why Mao should have expected anything different. He should have remembered the fierce intellectual debates of the 1930s concerning the path which China should follow. The whole area of intellectual freedom was widely discussed and such debate intensified in Yanan in the early 1940s. It should have been obvious that the debates would continue after 1949. But Mao did not see things in the same light. Since he himself believed that Communism was the only conceivable way forward, he seems to have felt that everyone would agree that, with a little refining here and there, China had now achieved the best possible blueprint for the future. But now the intellectuals had once again proved a disappointment. The launch of the Anti-Rightist Movement in the summer of 1957 marked the end of any faith Mao may ever have had that the intellectuals would help to bring about the technical revolution which China so desperately needed.

The Anti-Rightist Movement was launched with ferocious attacks on intellectuals from all walks of life. But the prime targets, as always, were the writers. Following in the old Confucian tradition, many of them had written works critical of the government and of officialdom. In ancient China many upright officials sent memorials to the Emperor to point out injustices. Some were listened to, whilst others were despatched by horrible means for their temerity. Yet others simply had their advice rejected and these were then free to retire to a hermit-like existence as a form of protest. In Mao's China that kind of opting out was not permitted. Once the intellectuals had been found wanting, the next move was to re-educate them. At least half a million intellectuals were 'sent to the countryside', *Xiafang* as it is called in Chinese, or sent to work in factories to teach them the glories of labour. The conditions were often truly appalling. Life in the Chinese countryside has never been easy, but in many parts of the country the climate is very harsh, and for those intellectuals who were used to a comparatively comfortable urban life it was hell. They were made to perform the most menial tasks in order to teach them humility, and the favourite punishment was to put them in charge of cleaning lavatories or mucking out pigsties. Not only they but their families also suffered – another old Chinese tradition. Many suffered a large salary cut, leaving barely anough for subsistence. Children who were branded as the offspring of a 'Rightist' were doomed both at school and as far as any future educational and job prospects were concerned. Many spouses divorced each other, sometimes to protect the one who had not been labelled a rightist, and sometimes to protect themselves against guilt by association. Many of those sent to labour in the wilds stayed there until after the death of Mao nearly twenty years later. Ironically, as one or two of them have told me, having been labelled during that particular campaign sometimes proved to be an advantage when the Cultural Revolution erupted in 1966. Already labelled as the dregs of society some (but by no means all) were spared further persecution. And if they were already doing hard labour in some remote region, then they were isolated from further attacks.

A whole string of well-known writers were attacked during the Anti-Rightist period, including Ding Ling and Liu Binyan. Ding Ling had always shown an interesting mixture of political opportunism and genuine enthusiasm for the Party, and had not hesitated to attack her own colleagues in earlier movements. None the less, her twenty-year period in the political wilderness, partly spent doing labour reform and partly spent in prison, was harsh in the extreme. Small wonder that when she was finally rehabilitated she was content to become one of the new establishment. One person who displayed greater backbone was the novelist and journalist Liu Binyan. He also came under severe attack, but even after his rehabilitation he has continued to be the scourge of the current leadership, and a major campaigner for greater political freedom and human rights. Although writers were primary targets scientists also came under attack. The now-famous dissident physicist Fang Lizhi had just graduated and was set for a brilliant career. However, as a nuclear physicist, he was assigned to work on the bomb and, as he told me in March 1989, his conscience would not allow him to do so. He made his views clear, and so became a victim of the campaign.

One lunatic and terrifying aspect of any Chinese campaign is the numbers game. The Three-Antis and Five-Antis Movements are good examples of the obsession with numerical labels. During the Anti-Rightist campaign, as a result of a casual remark by Mao Zedong, it was decreed that although 95 per cent of intellectuals were good, some 5 per cent were Rightists. Such a glib numerical statement gave rise to terrible injustices. If 5 per cent of the intellectuals were Rightists, then 5 per cent had to be dug out and exposed. Few officials had the courage to say that the factory, enterprise, school, university or whatever was in their charge did not contain any Rightists, or only contained 1 per cent, for they might then appear to be lacking revolutionary fervour. So the 5 per cent had to be found, even in enterprises where intellectuals were in very short supply and where the proletariat made up the vast majority of the employees. So old scores were settled and petty disputes remembered as people were labelled and condemned to years of bleakness. No one was accused through due legal process and, as a group of lawyers told me, they could not even save themselves, much less anyone else. Many of the injustices committed at that time were put right over twenty years later, but in the meantime the Chinese leaders had destroyed the confidence of the very sector of Chinese society which could have been so useful in building up the country. And, no less importantly, they had destroyed the happiness and the family life of so many people.

It was in this climate of leftism that Mao was able to launch the Great Leap Forward. The leadership was agreed that there had to be an improvement in agricultural output. The question was, how? Mao Zedong was still committed to the idea of mass mobilisation, whilst other leaders like Chen Yun preferred the idea of material incentives for the peasants, and the harnessing of expertise. The Anti-Rightist campaign had severely dented the latter aim, as so many experts were now in disgrace. These factors combined to facilitate the mobilisation of millions of people to build irrigation facilities during the winter of 1957–58. The drawback was that by taking so many people away from agricultural production, output of grain was going to suffer. What was needed, in Mao's view, was a much greater collectivisation of all aspects of rural life. This flew directly in the face of Soviet orthodoxy, which decreed that mechanisation must come before full collectivisation. But Mao knew the primitive state of the Chinese countryside, and decided that if China were not to achieve full collectivisation until it had mechanised, then it would never do so. Mao's solution was the People's Communes.

The communes were to be the heart and soul of China's social and agricultural development until the agricultural reforms of the late 1970s paved the way for their eventual disbandment in the 1980s. They were utopian. Families would no longer act as individual units, but would become an indivisible part of a much greater whole. The commune would take care of every aspect of the individual's life, from food supply to health care, from education to future employment. Each commune was to be a self-sufficient unit in a country which would be made up of similar self-sufficient units. The communes were an economic, an administrative and a social unit all rolled into one. Even in a small country, the concept that thousands of years of social tradition could be swept away overnight is startling enough, but in a country the size of China it was extraordinary. Although the commune system did not extend to the remote regions for several years to come, vast areas of the country were quickly communised. People were not consulted on this cataclysmic change in their lives. It was a decision by fiat.

Initially the communes were far too big, and by 1962 the original 25 000 had subdivided to become 75 000. The family was no longer considered necessary, since the commune would provide everything. Children were put into commune schools to free both parents for productive labour. There would be commune canteens, so people would not have to waste time going home to cook. The needs of every individual would be taken care of by the commune, so the old structure of family and family networks would be destroyed for ever.

That was the theory, but despite the mistaken Western view that the Chinese lack individualism, they came to hate the sudden destruction of their traditional family units. Release from the drudgery of preparing meals was not greeted with cries of joy, and as the communal mess halls were often inconveniently far away and the food unappetising, backsliding soon started. I recently asked the great Chinese anthropologist, Fei Xiaotong, how it had been possible to impose the commune system on a society in which, or so one had always been led to believe, the family unit was of central importance. He replied that the Chinese family had traditionally been a productive and reproductive unit, in which affection played a very secondary role, and in which the authoritarian family head had great power. The commune system was an extension of that model, and as long as the commune leader, like the family head, could successfully organise the people's lives and provide them with food, then they would accept the new pattern. But when he failed in that role, the trouble started. Because the communes swept away patterns of producing, marketing and distributing rural produce which had evolved over centuries, the utopian dream which replaced them caused such a dislocation of economic life that trouble was inevitable.

Mao's decision to speed up collectivisation was not a sudden aberration. It was the culmination of a long reassessment of the proper future path for China. Even in the days when China adopted the Soviet model more wholeheartedly, there had still been debate about its applicability to China, with the latter's huge rural base. China's leaders were increasingly confident of their ability to rule their leviathan in their own way, and were desperately anxious to speed up agricultural and industrial output. But another factor had entered the equation, and that was the direction in which Mao thought the USSR was going. In Mao's view it was definitely downhill. Although China's foreign relations will be discussed in another chapter, the increasing antagonism between Mao and Nikita Krushchev should be noted as an important spur to China's development in the late 1950s. The first major crack had shown up in 1956 when, without consulting the Chinese 'younger brother', Krushchev had delivered a swingeing attack on Stalin's memory at the Twentieth Congress of the Communist Party of the Soviet Union. Mao, despite the uneasy relationship which he had had with Stalin, admired him as a strong leader. Furthermore, Mao watched with growing mistrust the improvement in relations between the USSR and the USA. His conclusion was that the USSR was going down the 'revisionist road', and the Hungarian uprising in 1956 convinced him that there was a real crisis in the socialist camp. He greatly feared that unless he did something, China might go the same way. Hence the hasty creation of the People's Communes and the disastrous Great Leap Forward.

The aim of the Great Leap was to utilise underemployed labour power to make up for the lack of capital inputs. Wildly ambitious goals were set — China was to overtake Britain in steel production in fifteen years. Since the 'experts' could not be relied on, as proved by the Hundred Flowers Movement, then the enthusiasm of the masses would have to be harnessed. There was to be a reliance on both traditional and iconoclastic methods of production. The great steel works were to continue production, but the peasants would also start their own backyard steel furnaces. Never mind whether this projected upsurge would create bottlenecks. They could worry about that later.

It should be noted that with few exceptions the Chinese

leadership supported Mao's launching of the Great Leap Forward. Liu Shaoqi and Deng Xiaoping were in agreement on it, and even the normally cool Zhou Enlai later admitted to having been carried away. Chen Yun's was the sole rational voice. Chen, as mentioned earlier, believed in a rational and planned approach, and in 1956 he had warned against the over-hasty economic development which was already manifesting itself in a growth rate of 11 per cent. The Defence Minister, Peng Dehuai, was also unhappy, but less because he was against the philosophy of the communes and the Great Leap than because he still had faith in the Soviet model. As a military man he admired the professionalism of the Soviet Red Army. Mao Zedong's view was that the Chinese People's Liberation Army (PLA) should still be a guerrilla army, close to the people, although Mao was also firmly committed to the idea that China should develop its own nuclear capability, and indeed the USSR had signed an agreement with the Chinese to help them develop such a capability.

But Mao and Peng Dehuai had been at odds since the Korean War, and the knowledge that the PLA was to be engaged in agriculture and dyke-building rather than practising military manoeuvres fuelled Peng's anger. A further pin-prick was that Mao had already moved the master war tactician Lin Biao into a position in the Politburo which outranked Peng's. Peng knew 'that the writing was on the wall.

Before exploring the madness that was the Great Leap Forward, it is worth looking at the role which Deng Xiaoping was playing at that time. At the time of writing this book, Deng is still China's most senior leader, after an extraordinarily chequered career of political ups and downs. Before the massacre in Tiananmen Square in June 1989, for which Deng must be held largely responsible, he had been hailed by the outside world as a pragmatic liberal, the man who was taking China down the road towards capitalism, the market economy, free speech, and making the Chinese 'more like us'. But anyone who had followed Deng's career over the decades knew that whilst he might be a pragmatist in economic matters, he was far from being a liberal ideologue, as events in the summer of 1989 confirmed. A later chapter will explore Deng's triumphs and disasters in the 1980s, but where did he stand in the 1950s? His viewpoint then sheds a great deal of light on his actions thirty years later.

The son of a landlord Deng was born in Sichuan, China's most populous province in the south-west. Both mountainous and fertile, it is as famous for its fiery food as for the revolutionaries it has spawned. Deng was one of the group which studied in France, where he spent far more time learning about the Communist movement than about Western culture. Deng made the Long March and had played a vital role as the Political Commissar of the Second Field Army. Tough and abrasive, Deng has always believed in expertise, and was the author of the much-quoted remark that 'it doesn't matter if a cat is black or white. If it catches mice it's a good cat'. But Deng is no intellectual liberal, and when the Anti-Rightist Campaign was launched, Deng was right behind Mao. He may have appreciated the expertise of those who criticised the Party, but he did not view with equanimity the attack on the political system which he had helped to build. Although he later admitted that the Anti-Rightist Campaign had been applied too widely, he still maintained that it had been necessary. When the Great Leap was launched Deng was certainly a member of Mao Zedong's inner circle, and as head of the Party Secretariat Deng played a major role in the implementation of the Leap. He had much to gain in power and prestige if the Leap succeeded, as had Liu Shaoqi.

But even before the Great Leap was fully under way, trouble was brewing. Already the peasants were reporting food shortages in some areas. The harvest in 1958 had been excellent but so many peasants had been diverted to other work such as irrigation schemes, urban industry and even the new rural industries that the grain was not fully harvested. A belief that there was going to be a bumper harvest meant that in some areas officials had handed out free grain to the commune members. Peasants in various parts of China have told me that this made them think that the harvest was no longer their responsibility, and crops such as sweet potatoes were simply left to rot. This was a time of wildly inflated production targets. Although only 5.35 million tons of steel had been produced in 1957, the target for 1959 was 30 million tons. Even Mao felt that the targets should be lowered, and they were, but not enough.

To achieve the unreachable steel target, peasants were encouraged to set up 'backyard steel furnaces' to augment output. Since peasants were eating in mess halls they were pressured into melting down their superfluous cooking pots and many gladly made the sacrifice for the cause. Frequently, houses were pulled down and the timbers used for the furnaces. Whilst the peasants' enthusiasm was not in dispute, their expertise certainly was. Travellers passing through China during the late 1950s paint vivid pictures of looking out through train windows in the darkness, and seeing the rural landscape dotted by thousands of small steel furnaces, with tired, eager peasants desperately trying to live up to the slogan of the day — 'more, better, faster'. They may have produced it faster, but the amount of steel produced was minimal and of very poor quality. But even had it been of excellent quality, no one had thought how to transport it around the country to where it was most needed. China's infrastructure is still poor, and at that time it was far worse. And it was not only in steel production that enthusiasm proved the death of common sense. The grain quotas were also ludicrously high. Local leaders pledged to produce quantities of grain tens and even hundreds of times greater than their land had ever been known to produce before. Experimental plots were planted with the best seed grain, doused with fertiliser, and watched over day and night. Naturally their yields were high, and it was incorrectly interpreted that what one could get out of an experimental fraction of a hectare simply had to be multiplied up to get the production figure for a large area of land. Mao's call to plant more closely required more seed, and his dictum that ploughing should be deeper ruined the soil. Huge amounts of fertiliser were applied, with disastrous results.

At the same time there was a mass campaign to destroy birds, as they ate the grain. For days and nights no bird had a moment's rest. People shouted and banged saucepan lids until the birds fell dead with exhaustion. Then China reaped its silent spring, for those insects which would have been devoured by the birds, now devoured the crops.

It seemed as though a madness had gripped the country. Foreigners who visited China at the time said that the fervour was extraordinary. People seemed prepared to work like the possessed for weeks at a time. Terrible strains were put on people and equipment. If a man could work ten times as hard, then so could a boiler. No engineer wanted to be accused of backsliding, so when an ignorant bureaucrat told him to step up the pressure, he did so. There were many tales of equipment simply blowing up, and then production had to stop for days whilst it was being mended.

Even if they had doubts about the targets which they had set, no one wanted to be accused of 'right conservatism', and this is what caused the subsequent disaster. Pledges of enormous grain targets were coming in from all the provinces, prompting a steep escalation in the government's grain procurement quotas. Even if the targets seemed improbable, everyone wanted to believe in them. The pressure to fudge the figures was irresistible. Just as in the 1980s Chinese journalists were told to write about 'the good sides of the reforms', so during the Great Leap Forward statisticians doctored the figures 'to reflect great success' rather than the truth. Those who had the courage to protest about the lies were immediately accused of, at best, lacking the right attitude, and at worst of being a counter-revolutionary. The honest officials merely exaggerated the real production figures by a third or so, but many doubled and trebled the numbers, and very few people had the courage to point out that the Great Leap success story was a gossamer web that was about to break. Mao himself always had infinite faith in the power of mass mobilisation. But even Mao was beginning to see the danger signals, and to worry that the cadres might be pushing the people too far, and might be guilty of 'left deviation'. But now the movement had a momentum of its own, and the rural cadres, free from the supervision of the urban experts whom they had always resented, would not stop their lemming-like rush to disaster.

Although it was clear that matters were getting out of control, a number of additional events diverted the attention of the Chinese leaders from the impending crisis. In the spring of 1959 there was a revolt in Tibet, and although it was swiftly crushed it took the leadership by surprise, and the problems of both domestic and international fall-out occupied them during the next few months. Then the increasingly sharp disagreement between China and the Soviet Union took another turn. During the summer Defence Minister Peng

Dehuai had had a meeting with Krushchev whilst visiting Warsaw Pact countries. Although we do not know what went on between the two men, it is likely that Peng may have expressed dismay about the communes and the Great Leap Forward. But whatever happened, soon after Peng returned to China in June, Krushchev made his first public criticism of the commune system and, even more crucially, cancelled the agreement under which the USSR was to provide China with technical aid to develop a nuclear deterrent. Whatever Peng may or may not have said to Krushchev, Mao certainly thought that he had colluded with the Russians.

Peng Dehuai was of peasant origin and during a tour of the provinces had witnessed at first hand the falsification of the grain figures and the neglect of agriculture. He summed up his anguish in the following poem:

> The millet is scattered all over the ground
> The leaves of the sweet potato are withered.
> The young and the strong have gone to smelt iron
> To harvest the grain there are children and old women.
> How shall we get through next year?
> I shall agitate and speak out on behalf of the people.

And he did. He wrote a private letter to Mao, which the latter chose to publish, so bringing the fight out into the open. Towards the end of July, at the famous Party conference held at the mountain resort of Lushan, Mao counter-attacked, accusing Peng of 'right opportunism'. He asked, with some justification, why Peng had not spoken up at the time when even Mao himself was anxious about the Leap going badly off course? Mao felt that Peng had diverged so far from acceptable behaviour between Party members that he and his supporters would have to go through a period of 'rectification'. In September Peng was stripped of his post as Minister of Defence, and Lin Biao took over.

After this Mao hastened the Great Leap along with even greater intensity, although he knew that there were already great problems. One can only suppose that Mao was so angered by Peng's criticism that a perverse determination not to acknowledge by even a hair's breadth that Peng may have been right made him push even further along the road to catastrophe.

The ensuing calamity affected not only the peasants of China, but the Party and the leadership as well. The Lushan conference marked a turning point in the way disagreement was handled amongst the leadership. For whilst there had often been disputes, it had been possible to speak out without instant dismissal. But Peng's treatment at Lushan changed all that. New battle lines were being drawn, new coalitions formed, and the results would be destructive.

Although it would be several years before the political consequences made themselves felt, the concrete results of the Great Leap manifested themselves in 1960. Famine stalked the land. It was caused by a combination of circumstances. The huge harvests which local leaders had promised proved to be a chimera. In some areas the land had not even been planted, because it was reckoned that there would not be enough storage space for the expected surplus. The problem was compounded by very bad weather. Then in the summer of 1960 the Soviet Union withdrew the several thousand technical advisers who were in China. This marked the final point in the simmering Sino-Soviet dispute. The technicians were very important in many key technical programmes, and their departure contributed to the economic difficulties, and again distracted the leaders' attention from the problems of the peasants.

The famine was probably the worst the world has known this century. It is impossible to say how many people died because of the famine. However, the population dropped dramatically. Figures for the excess number of deaths over births vary from 15 million to 50 million, but it is certainly a minimum of 20 million. People were eating the bark off trees, grass and roots, many of which were poisonous. An official report said 'The people are too hungry to work and the pigs are too hungry to stand up.' Whole villages suffered from swollen limbs. Many local leaders, afraid of being accused of 'rightism' concealed the extent of the horror, and continued to maintain that the situation was 'excellent'. Not all areas suffered equally, but those which traditionally had poor farming conditions or were least developed tended to suffer most. In some areas infant mortality rose by 60 per cent and the fertility rate dropped by 20 per cent.

The famine is still a very sensitive subject in China. Although the Chinese government is now quite open about the devastating effects, local officials are much less so. In the northern

Province of Shandong, which I knew had been very hard hit, I recently tried to find an area which had suffered badly. But despite being taken to what must then have been a very poor locality, I came up against a wall of figure-fudging. Mao himself had admitted that the situation in Shandong was 'grave', but local officials were still assuring me that grain production had doubled during the famine years and that no one had starved. They assured me that Shandong had always been a successful grain-growing area, which is certainly not the case.

In 1981 the Chinese published statistics for grain production during 1960 and 1961 which indicate the gravity. Although Chinese statistics are frequently unreliable if they are aimed at discrediting the period to which they are referring, it is only too likely that in this case they are correct. Agricultural output in 1960 was apparently only 75.5 per cent of the 1958 output, and it dropped again in 1961. There was also a sharp decline in both light and heavy industrial output in the 1960–62 period. It was not only the rural but also the urban populations which suffered, although not as badly. But the grain ration in the cities was sharply reduced, and for a people who rely on grain as their staple food to the extent to which the Chinese did then, the reduction to one small bowl of rice was a considerable shock. There were long food queues in the cities. Interestingly, though, a Chinese friend who was a small girl at the time told me that many Chinese, herself included, were proud to make the sacrifice that was being asked of them. But others must have asked what was the advantage of a Communist government if it could not prevent the same terrible starvation which they had suffered under the Nationalists?

When the full extent of the economic and human tragedy became known, questions were naturally asked as to how it could have happened. Mao, with his usual wiliness pushed the blame on to others. An expert in formulating rash economic policies, he now disclaimed responsibility by saying that he was no economist and if the economic experts said that such targets were possible, who was he to contradict them? To an extent that is true, as Mao had generally only claimed expertise in the future path of the revolution for China, and in agriculture. But since Mao did know about things agricultural he must have realised that, with all the revolutionary fervour in the world, the outrageously exaggerated grain targets could not possibly have been reached. Mao cannot be apportioned all the blame, as the other leaders were also culpable, but it is possible that seeing the treatment meted out to Peng Dehuai, no one wanted to jeopardise his position by speaking up.

Now the time had come to pick up the broken pieces of industry and agriculture and restore the faith of the battered population in the Party. And the Party's credibility was certainly badly dented. Party leaders had initiated the catastrophe, and Party cadres had seen that it ran its course. Mao's prestige had suffered, and he was forced to accept some damage limitation. Already in 1959 Mao had given up his position as State Chairman to Liu Shaoqi, and now, in true Olympian style, Mao left the other leaders to repair the damage. Mao still retained his faith in mass mobilisation, but most of his colleagues did not, and from then on Deng Xiaoping was at odds with Mao over the strategy for recovery. Mao thought that the country would soon be on the road to recovery; Deng, Liu Shaoqi and Chen Yun, on the contrary, felt that a long period of recuperation would be needed. In 1962 Mao retreated to the 'second line', and spent several months in the city of Wuhan in central China, plotting the next steps for China. Meanwhile, back in Peking, almost all the policies of the Great Leap were being reversed and once again the emphasis was on expertise. Industrial enterprises were to be efficient, and the inefficient small plants were to be done away with. The peasants were to be given material incentives to restore their enthusiasm, and in some areas the commune system was dismantled until the situation improved.

To combat the general feeling of demoralisation, there was a relaxation on the cultural front as well. People were no longer restricted to the arid fare of stories, plays and operas about model Party cadres, and the old operas were revived. These were full of colourful but shamelessly 'feudal' characters such as princesses and heroic generals.

Meanwhile, Mao smouldered, and in August of 1962 there was a major meeting at which there was a titanic clash between the two separate approaches. The more pragmatic element of the leadership, men such as Deng Xiaoping, Liu Shaoqi and Chen Yun, felt that in order to dig China out of the morass into which it had slipped there had to be a different approach. Peasants needed material incentives; they should be allowed private plots on which to grow food. The extremes of the commune system had brought disaster, and must be toned down.

To Mao this approach was heresy, and he was already making the moves that would get him back into the thick of political decision-making. He was gathering about him a group of like-minded individuals. One was his wife, Jiang Qing, who had begun to play a more active role since 1959. She was severely critical of what she saw as the backsliding on the cultural front. She wanted to proletarianise Chinese opera, and other aspects of the arts. She had already made suggestions to the Ministry of Culture, but these were treated with contempt by the leaders of the cultural and propaganda fields, for which they were to pay dearly a few years later. But gradually Jiang Qing got together a group of kindred spirits, including the literary critic Yao Wenyuan, who had risen up the hierarchy as a result of his criticism of errant intellectuals during the Anti-Rightist campaign, and Zhang Chunqiao. Zhang had risen through posts in the Party and the journalistic field in Shanghai and by 1962 wielded considerable power in Shanghai in the realms of ideology, literature, the arts and education. These three people would eventually be three quarters of the notorious Gang of Four, which was swiftly given the name 'The Shanghai Mafia'. More sinister than any of them was another member of the clique, Kang Sheng. Trained in security tactics in the Soviet Union in the 1930s, Kang was responsible for public security. He was also a master in the Stalinist technique of fostering suspicion in Mao's mind about the loyalty of other leaders. He came from the same town as Jiang Qing, and had known her even before she went to Yanan.

And where did Defence Minister Lin Biao stand at this time? He was playing a very clever waiting game. To counteract the demoralisation which the Great Leap had caused amongst the troops, he increased political study in the army. As most of the soldiers were semi-literate peasant boys, Lin had them study a simplified version of Mao Zedong's Thought, the *Quotations of Chairman Mao*, which eventually became known as the *Little Red Book*. Lin gradually increased Party membership amongst the armed forces; he slowly moved his own supporters into the Ministry of Defence and he augmented the number of men who held dual military and civilian posts in the provinces. This was not to increase Party control over the military, but quite the reverse. In May 1965 Lin took the extraordinary step of abolishing all ranks in the PLA, and these were not officially restored until October 1988. It seemed to Mao that under Lin Biao the PLA combined the political and professional components that could make it a model for the whole country.

China was gathering momentum for another explosion. Mao was aware that time was not on his side. Although he still had over a decade to live, he felt that he was getting old, and his revolution was slipping through his fingers and being caught by those who he feared would rush it down the path of Soviet revisionism. He feared a resurgence of capitalism. He viewed with extreme anxiety the increasingly elitist educational system and thought that writers were not addressing themselves sufficiently to the needs of 'the masses', and were certainly not 'learning from the masses'.

In November 1965 the literary critic Yao Wenyuan wrote an article in a Shanghai journal. It was a criticism of a play written by the Deputy Mayor of Peking, Wu Han, called *Hai Rui Dismissed From Office*. To an outsider the article might simply have read as a somewhat vitriolic piece of literary criticism. But that piece of literary criticism marked the launch of the Great Proletarian Cultural Revolution.

CHAPTER THREE

THE CULTURAL REVOLUTION

What was the Cultural Revolution all about? Why did Mao launch a movement which was to prove so destructive even to those sectors of society which he championed? It has been argued that it was, quite simply, a power struggle. Certainly it turned into a power struggle between several factions, and in the process of it Mao purged many top leaders who he felt were taking China down the road to revisionist perdition. But it was much more than that, for it was also an attempt to change the soul of man.

Mao was convinced that China was sliding in the same direction as the Soviet Union, which he felt was controlled by an increasingly elitist and hidebound bureaucracy. In China he saw a widening gap between the leaders and the led. He had watched with great disquiet the reintroduction of a degree of private farming after the catastrophe of the Great Leap Forward. He knew that many Politburo decisions had been made and implemented without his consent. In the early 1960s he had seen a number of intellectuals once again daring to speak out against the suffocating Party control of the intellectual field. He saw the growth of an elite amongst the children of the Party leaders. Where in 1958 the majority of university entrants had come from peasant–worker backgrounds, now the majority came from intellectual or official backgrounds. Mao saw all this, and he also saw that he was growing old. If he wanted to leave a pure socialist society for posterity then he was going to have to act fast. He envisaged that, with sufficient support from the masses, within a year he would have transformed the teaching system, purged the

Party and the state and forged young successors in the purifying flame of revolution.

It may seem a little bizarre that a piece of literary criticism should have marked the beginning of a movement as cataclysmic as the Great Proletarian Cultural Revolution, as it was eventually to be known, but the Chinese are very familiar with historical allegory. Known picturesquely as 'pointing at the mulberry while upbraiding the ash', this has been a traditional Chinese method of attack. Wu Han, the author of the play, *Hai Rui Dismissed From Office*, was both a well-known literary figure and Deputy Mayor of Peking. For several years he had written about the upright official of the Ming dynasty, Hai Rui. Wu Han depicted Hai Rui as a champion of the masses, who pleaded the cause of the poor and oppressed before the Emperor and was dismissed for his pains. Immediately, Hai Rui was seen as an allegory for Peng Dehuai, who was dismissed from his post as Minister of Defence when he criticised the Great Leap Forward.

The Shanghai critic who launched the attack, Yao Wenyuan, was the son of a well-known writer. Yao the son had great literary aspirations, but lacked creative talent. He made up for this by attacking the works of better-known writers, and had consistently attacked 'rightist' literary figures. As mentioned in the previous chapter, he had climbed to fame in the 1950s over the assassinated reputations of other writers. He was very close to Mao's wife, Jiang Qing who, perhaps because of her earlier career in cinema and theatre, took an interest in matters 'cultural'. She found in Yao a perfect tool for her own attack on the cultural establishment.

Yao accused Wu Han of being ideologically unsound in idealising a 'feudal personality', whilst ignoring the more important class struggle of the masses against the Emperor, the bureaucrats and the landlords. Since Hai Rui had been an official in a dynasty which had ruled China some five centuries before the Communists took over, the expectation that he would have been well-versed in concepts of class struggle is academic, to say the least. But readers of Yao's article recognised that what Yao was attacking was not the Hai Ruis of yesterday, but the Hai Ruis of today, who also favoured a cautious approach to reform in order to mitigate social and economic upheaval.

With long experience in reading between the lines, readers
of Yao's article realised that Wu Han was not really the main
target of attack. The critical barb was actually being aimed at
Wu's boss, the Mayor of Peking, Peng Zhen. Peng was a Party
veteran who had worked with Liu Shaoqi in the 'white areas'
during the 1930s, and had taught at the Party school in
Yanan. After 1949 he increasingly emerged as the Chinese
Communist Party Central Committee's spokesman abroad.
He had worked closely with members of the Politburo such as
Deng Xiaoping, Liu Shaoqi and Chen Yun, who had a more
pragmatic approach to the economic development of China.
At the beginning of the Cultural Revolution he ranked ninth
in the Politburo, and so was a powerful national figure.

Mao was a master in the art of helping a man to dig his own
grave. As early as 1964 he had started to talk of the need for a
Cultural Revolution and had made Peng Zhen head of a
Cultural Revolution Group. But this was a very establishment
group, with only one radical amongst them. However, Mao
now called on Peng Zhen to initiate a thorough criticism of
Wu Han and his play. Peng tried to minimise Wu's errors as
'academic' rather than ideological and also suggested that the
Cultural Revolution should be conducted 'with the approval
of the leading bodies concerned'. Peng pleaded for 'gradual
reform' and 'peaceful debate'. In other words, the Party
groups would engage in some mild navel-gazing. This was not
at all what Mao had in mind. He wanted the Cultural
Revolution to be an all-out mass movement, and he called a
meeting to repudiate Peng Zhen and his report. Peng was
labelled as the number one enemy, and by the end of March
1966 had become the first major victim of the Cultural
Revolution. With Peng out, Mao dissolved the Peking Party
Committee, and his supporters were able to seize control of
the Party's propaganda machine and of the *People's Daily*.

In May 1966 the Cultural Revolution gained momentum
following a Party Central Committee meeting at which the
so-called 16 May Circular was approved. This reported the
dissolution of the old Cultural Revolution Group under Peng
Zhen, and the formation of a new one, which would be
directly under the Standing Committee of the Politburo. This
was an altogether more radical group, and was nominally
headed by Mao's amanuensis, Chen Boda.

On 26 May the first so-called *Dazibao* or Big Character Poster appeared. These posters were the hallmark of the Cultural Revolution, and were used for attack and counter-attack. The author of the first poster was Nie Yuanzi, Party Secretary of the Philosophy Department of Peking University, Beida. This revolutionary firebrand was not in her twenties or thirties, as one might expect, but a woman in her fifties. When her first husband was labelled a 'rightist' in the 1950s, she divorced him and married a high-ranking Party official. The poster which she pasted up on the Beida campus attacked the university authorities, and especially the President, Lu Ping. Characteristically, this clash between Nie and the university hierarchy had its origins in an earlier movement. Nie and a group of like-minded colleagues now accused Lu Ping and *his* colleagues of wanting to sabotage the Cultural Revolution. She charged them with neglecting politics and the study of Mao Zedong Thought; of reverting to traditional book-learning; of neglecting the importance of manual labour for students and staff; of concentrating on academic achievement and of favouring academically bright students.

It was precisely such characteristics of institutes of higher education that Mao deplored, so Nie Yuanzi's poster struck a resonant chord in the Chairman, if, indeed, it had not been directly inspired by Mao in the first place. When Mao specifically praised Nie's poster, the writing was on the wall for university administrators like Lu Ping, who was dismissed in June. That same month it was announced that schools and universities would be closed for six months, so that a new system of education could be worked out. Under the new system examinations would be scrapped, there would be greater concentration on ideology and manual labour and less on formal academic teaching, and students would be chosen for the purity of their class background, rather than for their academic attainment.

Mao had always been against formal education, and pointed to his own extremely haphazard education as an example of how much a person could achieve without years of formal learning. He castigated his niece, Wang Hairong, for not having the courage to stay away from class, and encouraged her to rebel against being assigned too much school work. He gave her the heady advice 'Just stay away and tell the others that you want to rebel against the school system.'

It was clear from the start of the Cultural Revolution that in addition to an overhaul of the educational structure Mao also wanted a complete shake-up of the cultural field, hence the attack on Wu Han's play. Mao's wife, Jiang Qing, was already waging a battle against the entrenched cultural bureaucracy and was revising traditional operas.

In order to accomplish this wholesale transformation of China Mao first had to get rid of those who would stand in the way of his grand plan. Mao was to say later on that he had already decided in January 1965 that the State Chairman, Liu Shaoqi would have to go, and Liu was Mao's major target as he launched the Cultural Revolution. And Mao did with Liu exactly what he had done with Peng Zhen. He let him destroy himself by his own actions. After Mao had signalled approval of Nie Yuanzi's poster at the end of May, he then made one of his customary disappearances, this time to Wuhan in central China.

Mao frequently used this technique during the Cultural Revolution. He would launch a new phase, and then disappear and let the opposing sides fight it out. He would then reappear and condemn the losers or praise the winners. Or he would publicly praise the winners, whilst already plotting the next move against them. The Chinese call this tactic 'Sitting on the mountain top watching the tigers fight', and Mao was an expert at it. In June 1966 Liu Shaoqi was supposed to be carrying out the aims of the Cultural Revolution to root out 'revisionism' and to attack those Party members 'taking the capitalist road'. But Liu instead sent large numbers of Work Teams to the universities to quell the unrest that Mao had fanned. Some 10000 Work Teams were sent not only to the universities but also to factories and Party organisations. In other words, Liu wanted the rectification to be carried out from above by the Party and state machinery itself. This was quite the reverse of Mao's vision of a mass movement from below.

Mao's reappearance could hardly have been more dramatic. On 16 July 1966 he made his historic swim in the Yangtse River at Wuhan. The widely publicised photo of their leader, fully clothed and accompanied by a fully clothed aquatic entourage, caused great excitement amongst the Chinese. And indeed, the spectacle of the seventy-two-year-old old Chinese Communist Party Chairman doing his own brand of swimming in one of the world's greatest rivers caused a stir around the world. Who cared that the current carried him swiftly downstream, so minimising the effort he had to make? It was a supremely successful public relations exercise. The Chinese all realised exactly what Mao was telling them – that he might be a septuagenarian, but he was fit and well and quite capable of leading China through a new revolution. Mao's return to Peking was as triumphant as that of any of the Caesars returning to Rome after a successful campaign.

In August the *de facto* demotion of Liu Shaoqi took place. The Central Committee held a meeting in Shanghai, packed with Mao's supporters. It put forward Mao's view that it was more important to strive for revolutionary purity than for economic success and all bureaucrats, intellectuals and Party members were to be subjected to 'class struggle'. Thus Mao managed to get a spurious Party sanction for the mayhem that he was unleashing. Liu was demoted to eighth position in the Politburo, whilst Defence Minister Lin Biao was promoted to second place. Liu Shaoqi must have known that the end was in sight for him when, only five days earlier, Mao had written his own famous Big Character Poster, entitled 'Bombard the Headquarters'. This attacked 'leading comrades' who during Mao's absence had 'encircled and suppressed revolutionaries and imposed a white terror'. It took no special political acumen to work out that Liu himself was the headquarters which were to be bombarded. Although Liu Shaoqi was the most important casualty amongst the top leaders, Deng Xiaoping and others were also the subjects of fierce criticism and became political outcasts.

It is often asked why Liu did not foresee what Mao would do, and did not use his considerable political machinery to counter-attack. Since Liu is now dead we do not know the answer, but he may have thought that after the disastrous Great Leap Forward Mao would never again launch a destructive mass movement. Liu was himself such a creature of the Party organisation that it may never have occurred to him that Mao would be prepared to destroy the very Party which he had played such a crucial part in establishing. But Mao had already worked out that if the Party were to be temporarily out of action, then something or someone else had to take its place, and that someone was he. A shamelessly adulatory campaign to praise Mao's infallibility and genius gathered momentum, and its most vigorous orchestrator was Minister of Defence, Lin Biao. Lin lauded Mao as the 'greatest genius for ten thousand years'. Although this excessive adulation was to be condemned in the years to come, there is no doubt that during the early months of the Cultural Revolution Mao found it very useful. As the Party waned in importance, so Mao became the focus of devotion. His picture was everywhere, his quotations were on every loudspeaker on the streets and even in trains. He was the 'Red sun in our hearts', the 'Greatest Marxist who ever lived', 'the Great Helmsman'. At the end of 1966 the reorganised Ministry of Culture announced that it was publishing 35 million copies of *The Selected Works of Mao Zedong*. Mao had often pondered the human need for a god or gods, and he was now exploiting that need to the full. When, in 1970, the American journalist Edgar Snow raised with Mao the Russian criticism that China had a cult of the individual, Mao agreed, but pointed out that the reason why Krushchev was ousted was probably because he had *no* cult of the individual.

Shortly after the Plenum that demoted Liu Shaoqi Mao put on a Red Guard armband, and before the end of August had held the first of the Red Guard rallies in that same Tiananmen Square in Peking where in 1949 he had declared the founding of the People's Republic of China. The rallies were to become a hallmark of the first year of the Cultural Revolution. Who were the Red Guards? The majority were teenage middle-school pupils, but university students who were slightly older also formed into Red Guard groups and factory workers formed their Worker Rebel groups. The first group of Red Guards appeared on the Peking University campus. Whilst Mao did not actually initiate the Red Guard movement, he quickly saw how he could exploit the revolutionary fervour of its young disciples.

The Red Guards were allowed to travel free on China's railways. They came to Peking from all over China, and they made this pilgrimage in their millions. It is estimated that some 11 million attended the vast rallies held in the Tiananmen Square between August and November, when the last rally took place. Peking reeled under the shock of the youthful influx, but people did their best to provide food, clothing and shelter for the Red Guards. Their one desire was to see Mao, and there was hysteria when he appeared on the viewing stand in front of the Imperial City. Film of the period shows a sea of young people waving red flags and Mao's *Little Red Book*, with tears streaming down their faces as they saw the incarnation of their socialist dream. A leading Red Guard, who was then only sixteen years old, told me that the emotional fervour was extraordinary. The Red Guards sang revolutionary songs for hours and shouted out Mao quotations. There was a terrible press of bodies when he appeared. She said that although he was a long way off, she was sure that his face glowed, and he seemed to her to be neither male nor female, but a god.

Lin Biao gave the main speech at the first Red Guard rally, and Jiang Qing opened the second rally. Both speeches fanned the Red Guard hysteria, and for the actress Jiang Qing this must have seemed the chance of a lifetime, with herself in the lead role and a cast of millions. It was during his meetings with Red Guards at this time that Mao made one of his most famous quotations. He said, 'The world is yours as well as ours, but in the last analysis it is yours. You young people, full of vigour and vitality are in the prime of your life, like the sun between eight and nine in the morning. All our hopes are placed on you.' This quotation was pasted up all over Peking.

But the Red Guards soon came to symbolise everything that was violent and anarchic. They split into numerous factions, often with an exclusivity based on the class background of the faction members. There were two main factions to be seen on the university campuses. Those students who came from an intellectual background, and who because of their family background tended to be academically excellent, formed one main faction. The other was formed by the children of officials and bureaucrats. These were usually less good academically, but had perfect class credentials and would expect to move swiftly up the official ladder after graduation. Each faction firmly believed that it had the monopoly of truth.

But before the Red Guards turned on each other, first of all they turned on the population. Their aim was to destroy the 'Four Olds'. These were old customs, old ideas, old culture and old habits 'of the exploiting classes'. Red Guards burst into people's houses and searched out anything that might be construed as being one of the 'Four Olds', and a great number of things fell into one of those categories. People watched helplessly as their possessions were destroyed. Bonfires were made of books which were considered reactionary, and any Chinese classic or work of foreign literature was a target. Any work on religion, any religious symbol, such as a statue of the Buddha or the Virgin Mary, was instantly destroyed or taken away for inspection. Records of classical music were smashed. 'Bourgeois' clothes were torn or burnt. The wanton destruction was appalling. Some of the things the Red Guards took away were restored to their owners several years later, but most were gone for ever. In a country like China, where many things were in short supply at that time, the loss of a record of a Beethoven symphony often caused more grief than the loss of an object of greater monetary value.

Temples, and places of cultural interest were prime targets for the young iconoclasts. In Tibet, many of the most sacred places of an age-old religion were desecrated and destroyed. Some of the sharper curators of museums and places of historic interest hastily concealed many valuable things, and did their best to minimise the damage. I remember when I first went to Peking in 1972, wandering through the long covered gallery at the Summer Palace and assuming that it was the Red Guards who had whitewashed over the delicate paintings. I found out later that the palace staff had done it in order to save them from worse depredations.

The destruction of China's cultural heritage during this time of state-sanctioned vandalism was almost unimaginable. Paintings of the Tang and Song dynasties were burnt; unique porcelain was casually smashed. Many of these precious things were owned by private individuals who had a deep appreciation of their culture and tradition but could do nothing to combat the young hooligans. As it was, the owners of such things were likely to be beaten up and humiliated, and if they pleaded for their possessions the Red Guards were even more vindictive.

Eventually, people who were considered to be living too bourgeois an existence had to give up part of their living space, and manage with one or two rooms where they originally had several. Before the Cultural Revolution a large number of people in Peking owned their own houses (and some of them have now been returned to their owners), but during the Cultural Revolution the concept of private ownership was anathema.

When one talks to people who suffered during the Cultural Revolution it is surprising to find how many of the professional classes lived a much more privileged existence than their counterparts in the West. It was not that they lived in luxurious houses (although many of the leadership did), but compared with most of the population they earned very good salaries, and it was not uncommon for professors at the more famous universities to have at least one servant, and sometimes several. Even at the height of the Cultural Revolution some of these families were allowed to keep one servant, although by that stage the servant in question had sometimes become so imbued with the revolutionary spirit that the family would have been happier without her. There are stories of *ahyi*, as they are called, spending all day at political meetings and only returning home in the evening to demand that their employers serve them dinner.

This kind of privileged existence was to be seen in many strata of Chinese society. Red Guard posters and pamphlets, and eyewitness accounts by Red Guards, tell of their amazement and fury when they burst into the house of a potential victim, who might be a high-ranking government cadre, to discover spacious, well-furnished rooms, luxurious carpets and beautiful artefacts. Nothing can justify the damage done by the Red Guards, but many of them who came from less privileged families must have felt that for a socialist society there was an unacceptable discrepancy between the leaders and the led.

The people who were natural targets for the Red Guards were Chinese who had spent a great deal of time abroad or who had at one time worked for foreign companies in China. Many of these, with no justification whatsoever, were labelled spies. One of the best accounts of the persecution of such a person is Nien Cheng's *Life and Death in Shanghai*. She and her husband had worked for a foreign oil company, and she lived in considerable comfort in a house full of beautiful Chinese porcelain, which the Red Guards destroyed. She was subjected to several 'struggle sessions' in which the victim was shouted at for hours on end to confess his or her crimes, often with some physical brutality as an accompaniment. But Nien Cheng was a woman of quite extraordinary resilience, and despite years of solitary confinement, brutal treatment and malnutrition in jail, she never succumbed to the temptation to write a false confession in order to end the persecution. Hers was by no means an isolated case.

People known to be religious believers were also prime targets. Priests, monks and nuns were badly harassed by the young dogmatists. Until the Cultural Revolution a number of churches and temples were still well attended. Although the Chinese Catholic Church had broken with the Vatican in 1958 there were still practising priests and nuns and a large number of believers in an independent Chinese Catholic Church. Because of the Catholic Church's former close ties with the Vatican its adherents were also easy targets. Many clergymen were jailed, adding to the numbers who had been imprisoned shortly after the Communist take-over. Gradually all the churches and temples were closed. Many were very badly damaged, and a number of the buildings took on a new mantle as they were turned into factories or machinery repair shops.

In a movement which combined revolutionary zealotry and xenophobia, the types of people described above were predictable victims. It is less obvious why so many members of the teaching profession were treated with such cruelty by their pupils. Although many university lecturers had studied abroad, and taught such suspect subjects as Western literature, a great number had not, yet they still came under attack. The acts of cruelty and degradation meted out by the Red Guards to lecturers and teachers were so atrocious that although one can suggest a number of contributing factors, even today I still find it largely unfathomable.

Teachers were made to stand in front of hundreds, sometimes thousands, of Red Guards, who would scream accusations at them. These ranged from 'putting marks in command' (giving top priority to academic attainment) to 'praising revisionist literature' to 'favouring gifted pupils', and many even less rational accusations. Teachers were made to wear dunces' hats; glue was smeared on their backs and posters stuck on to them with a list of their 'crimes'. At best they were made to perform menial tasks such as cleaning out the classrooms or the lavatories. At worst they suffered terrible beatings and torture. Many were made to kneel on broken glass. One incident which caused a shudder of horror in the early days of the Cultural Revolution happened at the girls' middle school attached to the Peking Normal (teachers) College. There the girls made the female president of the school crawl through a narrow drainpipe, and then they beat her to death. Anyone who has been to China and seen Chinese schoolgirls knows how much younger, shyer and more innocent they seem than their Western counterparts. Yet they had committed an act of appalling brutality. Why?

It is difficult to find anyone who can give an answer. Just as in Germany it is hard to find anyone who will admit to having supported Hitler's policies, so in China it is hard to find a Red Guard who will admit to having been a violent thug. Almost all in a certain age bracket were Red Guards, but they all say that it was 'the others' who committed the worst horrors. However, there are a few who admit to having beaten up people whom they regarded as class enemies, and felt that they were justified in doing so. They regarded these people as traitors to the revolutionary masses, people who were out to wreck the socialist ship of state on a revisionist sandbank. The very innocence of the Red Guards meant that their views and actions could easily be manipulated by the leftist radicals.

There is, however, another aspect, and that is the very Confucian nature of Chinese society. One manifestation of this is people knowing and accepting what they see as their proper place in society. There is a much greater respect for authority than in many societies. (More about whether that is now changing in a later chapter.) This applies particularly in the relationship between teacher and taught. Chinese schoolchildren and students show infinitely more respect for their teachers than they do in the West, and anyone who has visited a Chinese school has been both impressed and possibly made slightly uncomfortable by the seeming lack of spontaneity. It has always struck me as completely unnecessary, for instance, that children should sit with their arms crossed *behind* their backs when they are not writing or holding a book. It must be so uncomfortable that I wonder they can concentrate at all.

There is also the aspect of mass hysteria and mob violence which needs to be taken into account when considering Red Guard violence. Any mob can work itself up to a pitch where it commits acts of extraordinary violence and cruelty, and there is no reason why a mass of Chinese teenagers should be any different. A group of teenagers who were usually constrained by their parents, their teachers or the Communist Party Youth League must have felt as though for the first time in their lives they could breathe freely, and the lifting of all restraints had a devastating effect. But one should also not lose sight of the fact that many of them really believed that they were right.

It was the Red Guards who broke the fingers of a famous pianist because he played 'reactionary' music (Chopin and so on). They broke the legs of a famous playwright, and many other well-known figures in the cultural field suffered at their hands. One of the most tragic victims was the writer Lao She, famous throughout the world for his novel *Rickshaw Boy*. The Red Guards beat him so terribly that he was battered and bleeding . There is still some mystery about his death. Some say that the Red Guards threw him into one of Peking's lakes and drowned him, but an eyewitness told me that after a particularly brutal beating he himself walked into the lake, surrounded by thousands of Red Guards, and drowned. There is no doubt that the Red Guards planned that he should die, one way or the other. Yet he was a writer who had always been a champion of the poor and the oppressed.

Lao She was only one of thousands of people who committed suicide during the Cultural Revolution. Although there are no exact figures, when the Gang of Four were put on trial in 1980 they were accused of having persecuted more than 700 000, of whom 35 000 were persecuted to death. But other estimates are much higher, and it is likely that at least 400 000 people died, and millions more suffered persecution. Scarcely a single Chinese, whether victim or persecutor, was untouched by the Cultural Revolution, and many will never recover from the trauma. To the Chinese, for whom 'face' or the loss of it is so important, the public humiliation of having to stand in front of one's peers, and be ritually humiliated by Red Guards young enough to be one's children was unbearable. Many said that they could stand the physical cruelty

(Top) Looking over Tiananmen Square, Mao Zedong declares the founding of the People's Republic of China on 1 October 1949
(Bottom) Mao Zedong and his wife, Jiang Qing, studying in the spring of 1949

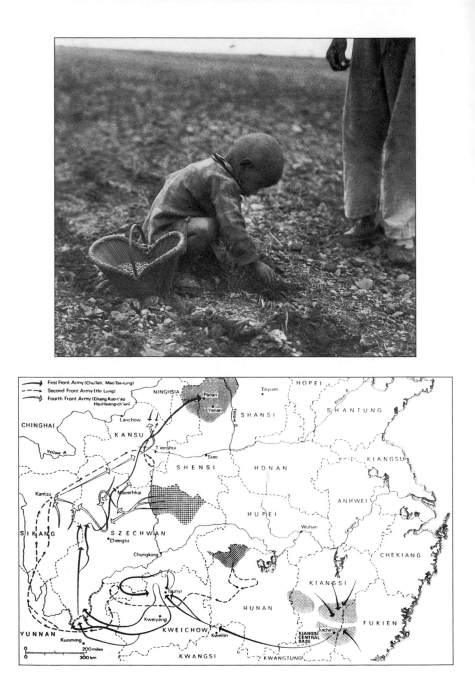

(Top) Rural poverty before 1949
(Bottom) Route of the Long March

(Top) 'China–Soviet friendship will safeguard peace' (woodcut by Li Hua, 1950)
(Bottom) Mao Zedong, Stalin and Krushchev in Moscow on the occasion of
Stalin's 70th birthday in December 1949

(Top) Woodcut showing peasants constructing a cement factory during the Great Leap Forward
(Bottom) Reading quotations from Mao before beginning agricultural work during the Cultural Revolution

(Background) Ecstatic Red Guards cheer Mao Zedong during the Cultural Revolution
(Top) Mao Zedong, Prime Minister Zhou Enlai and Defence Minister Lin Biao
acknowledging the Red Guards
(Bottom) Red Guards parade a government official through the streets wearing a
dunce's hat

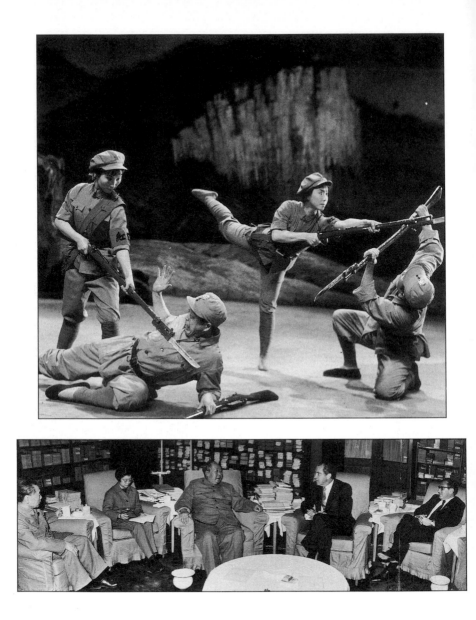

(Top) The Red Detachment of Women – a 'model' revolutionary ballet from the
Cultural Revolution period
(Bottom) Mao Zedong and Zhou Enlai receive President Richard Nixon and
Henry Kissinger in February 1972

(Top) Zhou Enlai lying in state in January 1976
(Bottom) Mao Zedong lying in state in September 1976

(Top) Mao Zedong's widow, Jiang Qing, at her trial in 1980
(Bottom left) Effigies of Jiang Qing and fellow Gang of Four member, Zhang
Chunqiao after their fall from power in 1976

much better than the humiliation, which was an emotional flaying. A number of these victims viewed the future with despair, and decided that they no longer wanted to be a part of it.

Not only were teachers, writers and cultural figures prime targets, but top-ranking officials too. One of the most famous was the Foreign Minister Chen Yi, a doughty revolutionary veteran. As Foreign Minister he was responsible for having sent in Work Teams to the various institutes under the auspices of the Foreign Ministry, such as the Foreign Languages Institute, so he was an early victim when Mao rounded on the Work Teams. He was subjected to several 'struggle sessions', made to write a confession (which he later repudiated) and to wear a dunce's hat. Chen was a tough old man, and insisted on continuing to wear the dunce's hat because, he said, he had grown to like it. But despite his dogged refusal to succumb to the harassment, Chen Yi was never the same man again.

Another victim of a particularly vicious attack was the wife of Liu Shaoqi, the elegant, American-educated Wang Guangmei. She had been in charge of the Work Teams sent to the most famous science university in China, Qinghua (Tsinghua). The attacks started in December 1966, and a few months later there was a 'struggle session' against her at Qinghua that left a particularly bad taste in the mouth. She was made to wear stiletto-heeled shoes and a *cheongsam*, the traditional high-necked, close-fitting dress, with a string of ping-pong balls around her neck to represent a string of pearls which she used to wear. One felt that it was Jiang Qing's envy of the attractive Wang Guangmei which had prompted this type of attack. Wang Guangmei was a very successful ambassadress for China when she accompanied her husband on state visits, and one of the accusations flung at her was her 'shameless' behaviour in dancing with President Sukarno whilst she and her husband were visiting Indonesia. There seems to have been a convenient amnesia about the impromptu dances in which the Communist Party leaders indulged whilst in the caves of Yanan, or the dances in the Peking Hotel after the Communists took power, at which Zhou Enlai was a star performer. But despite what she had to endure, Wang Guangmei survived, and after the fall of Jiang

Qing and her supporters in 1976, she was restored to political favour.

The last of the huge Red Guard rallies was held in November, and the Red Guards then roamed around the country 'learning from society', causing considerable disruption whilst they did so. No one dared to stop them from travelling free on the trains, and they crammed aboard for days of travel through the vast Chinese countryside. There were so many of them that no one could move. Those who had seats would not leave them for fear of never getting them back, and so urinated where they sat. Those standing could not get past the crowds of other Red Guards to get to the lavatories, which were crowded with other Red Guards, so they urinated where they stood. And in addition there was the added detritus which one gets on all Chinese trains – peanut shells, orange peel, watermelon seeds. They looked and smelled like travelling rubbish tips.

Now the workers and peasants were organised into groups of 'revolutionary rebels', and at the turn of the year the Party newspaper, the *People's Daily*, then under the control of the radicals, called on everyone to 'seize power from below'. They were told to take the French Revolution's Paris Commune as their model.

The Shanghai radicals, led by Zhang Chunqiao, Yao Wenyuan and Wang Hongwen took this encouragement at face value and launched a verbal assault on the municipal government and the Shanghai bureaucrats. Wang Hongwen had 'helicoptered' to power and fame, as the Chinese picturesquely express it. He had started as a security guard at the Number Seventeen Cotton Mill in Shanghai, and had shown great talent in arousing the revolutionary fervour of his fellow factory workers. Tall, good-looking and extremely articulate, he managed to rally large numbers behind Zhang Chunqiao, and his reward was to become the fourth member of the Gang of Four. In February Zhang, Yao and Wang declared the establishment of the Shanghai Commune. Zhang was the Chairman, Yao the Vice-Chairman. Triumphantly they sent Mao a telegram announcing the victory. But although Mao had lauded the Paris Commune as a model, he did not want to see it exactly replicated in China. When the Shanghai radicals arrived in Peking flushed with success, Mao berated them for what they had done, and said that the notion that government by the masses meant doing away with all leaders was 'extreme anarchism'. The Paris Commune lasted for seventy-two days, the Shanghai Commune a mere seventeen.

Having declared that there could not be an absence of leaders, Mao now made it clear what kind of leadership structure he wanted to see. Revolutionary Committees were to be formed based on a 'three-way alliance' of the army, the masses and those cadres of the old bureaucracy who were still acceptable. This ideal triumvirate proved extremely difficult to bring about. Many of the 'acceptable' cadres were people who had been brought down by the revolutionary rebel groups and after a period of 'struggle' and self-criticism had been reinstated. Now they were being asked to join hands with the very people who had attacked them. The radicals, for their part, were concerned that those reinstated cadres would merely bide their time and wait for an opportunity to take revenge against their former persecutors. And the third arm of the triumvirate, the army, where did it stand?

In China the People's Liberation Army, the PLA, was the most important force in bringing about the overthrow of the KMT government and the installation of a Communist government in 1949, but that did not mean that after the victory it wanted the civil war to continue. The PLA, like most armed forces, is inherently conservative in that it believes in an orderly society. The notion that unruly teenagers and rebellious factory workers should be the new masters of China was anathema to the PLA commanders. Although the PLA had been given orders towards the end of January 1967 to 'Support the Left', by the end of the summer the rebel groups had gained control in only six out of the twenty-nine provinces. The reason was quite straightforward. As a result of Lin Biao's gradual infiltration of military men into high Party posts throughout the regions, it was frequently the case that a man might be commander of a military region or district, and at the same time be the political commissar of the party organisation. So there he was, as military commander, being asked to help the rebels to smash the very Party organisation of which he was also a leader. Very few people are going to voluntarily engage in such an act of self-destruction.

In July 1967 a particularly bizarre event took place which

involved the powerful Commander of the Wuhan Military Region in central China, one Chen Zaidao. Chen had shown a deplorable lack of the the correct ideological orientation by backing a tough alliance of workers and militia against the Maoist groups in the city of Wuhan. So two members of the Cultural Revolution Group, Wang Li and Xie Fuzhi flew down from Peking to administer a stern rebuke. However, they were captured by the worker–militia alliance, known as 'The Million Heroes Army', and were badly roughed up. Zhou Enlai then flew down to rescue the two men, and narrowly escaped kidnap himself. But in one of those strange twists that characterised the Cultural Revolution, although Chen Zaidao was taken to Peking, criticised and made to study the works of Mao Zedong, nothing worse happened to him and he was eventually transferred to another military region. It seems likely that even the powerful Cultural Revolution Group feared a military backlash if Chen had been too severely punished.

Meanwhile the battle between the moderates and the radicals swung back and forth. In February and March Zhou Enlai and other Party veterans pleaded for moderation, and for the attacks on loyal cadres to cease. Mao was giving out his usual conflicting signals. One moment he would praise disorder, and the next would state virtuously that the battle must be fought with words, not with weapons. He would condemn anarchy, then once again fan revolutionary vigour.

By June there had been a huge purge of leading Party members. Zhou Enlai was having to run the State Council with only two vice-premiers, where previously there were fifteen; over half of the Central Committee members had been denounced; one third of the Politburo had been out of public view for nearly a year. There had been violence on a colossal scale in factories, and this had caused production in many vital areas to grind to a halt. There were reports of many deaths after armed clashes between groups of workers. This was a most alarming development, as the workers and Red Guard groups were now frequently very well armed. These were not home-made weapons (though they had those too), but machine guns and bazookas stolen from PLA arms depots. Another source of weapons for groups in the south of the country were the arms trains which were going to the

Sino-Vietnamese border with supplies for the Vietnamese troops to use against the United States. These were stopped and ransacked by workers and Red Guards, and the destruction which the opposing groups then wreaked upon each other was almost beyond imagining. An ex-Red Guard described to me the horror of seeing bloated and blackened corpses piled up in lorries which roared through the streets as the various factions exhibited their dead. Some factions stole corpses from their enemies in order to inflate their own casualty figures.

This is another of the many puzzles of the Cultural Revolution. The degree of violence which the Red Guards used against those who had always been in authority over them was sickening enough in its viciousness. But as the details began to leak out, what everyone both inside and outside China found impossible to believe were the horrors which the rival Red Guard and workers' groups visited upon each other. Some of the most graphic and disturbing accounts have come from the Red Guards themselves. They tortured each other. They beat each other to death. Girls were raped and murdered by Red Guards from rival groups. The victims were too numerous to name, but one of the best-known is Deng Pufang, son of the Chinese leader, Deng Xiaoping. He was a physics student at Qinghua University, which saw some of the worst violence. Since his father was a prominent leader who was under attack, the son was an obvious victim. Some accounts say that he was thrown from a fourth-floor window, and some say that he jumped to escape capture. Either way, the result was the same. Since that day he has been paralysed from the waist down.

One tends to think of the Cultural Revolution as an event which nearly destroyed China internally, and whilst this is true there was also considerable damage to its foreign relations. In the summer of 1967 the Foreign Ministry was taken over by a group of leftist radicals.The war in Vietnam had already inspired the Chinese to predict that it heralded a worldwide 'storm of revolution', and to proclaim the universality of the Cultural Revolution. Governments around the world which did not instantly show the same degree of enthusiastic support for the events in China were said to be opposing the wishes of their populations.

By August 1967 Red Guards in Peking had mounted mass

demonstrations outside embassies representing countries as varied in their political persuasions as Czechoslovakia and India, France and Mongolia. The most notable event was the burning down of the British mission in Peking, at that time still headed by a chargé d'affaires, and the seizing of the British Consulate in Shanghai, with physical assaults on their staff. The British were under attack because of their refusal to allow left-wing elements in Hong Kong to stage their own Cultural Revolution. Troublemakers had been arrested, and this led to a series of strikes in the colony, where there was rioting and violence. When the British authorities refused to give in to left-wing demands, China cut off the water supply to Hong Kong, which led to stringent rationing.

In Chinese embassies in various capitals around the world, Chinese students and militant diplomats demonstrated against the governments in whose capitals the embassies were based, and fought against the local police who tried to break up the demonstrations. Since all but one of the Chinese ambassadors had been recalled to Peking there was no restraining hand on the militants. Even countries normally friendly to China found this all too much, and many broke off relations.

Although the left-wingers in the Foreign Ministry appeared to target their attacks on foreign embassies, they really had their sights set on a much loftier prize – Prime Minister Zhou Enlai. They knew that he was a close ally of the disgraced Foreign Minister Chen Yi, and as China's former Foreign Minister and architect of China's foreign policy, the attacks on foreign embassies would cause acute embarrassment to Zhou. If he condemned them then they would label him a 'rightist' and 'anti-revolutionary' and if he said nothing, then he would be condemned by foreign governments. But the radicals reckoned without Mao Zedong.

Mao had been indulging in one of his strategic absences whilst the anti-foreign demonstrations had been going on, but now he roared back to Peking like a hurricane, and roundly condemned the behaviour of the leftists. They had gone too far. Their leader was arrested, and the PLA took over the Foreign Ministry to restore control. Mao was still sufficiently in touch with reality to realise that he could not afford to alienate the whole world, and he certainly could not afford to lose his most shrewd of allies, Zhou Enlai.

In October there were pleas for the young to go back to school, and whilst a few did, the majority continued to roam the country, enjoying the freedom which they may have sensed would never come again. It was a liberation of both the spirit and the body. They could say and do as they liked, and after years of discipline the freedom was intoxicating. Many Red Guards had affairs with each other, which would have been inconceivable under normal Chinese social conditions at the time. Many married each other, and those hastily contracted marriages often ended just as hastily when China regained a degree of normality.

At about this time the cracks began to appear in the alliance between Jiang Qing and Defence Minister Lin Biao. Lin had given her status and power by putting her in charge of cultural affairs in the PLA. He had supported her efforts to proletarianise Chinese opera. The two of them had fanned the Red Guard violence. But now the inherent incompatibility between the radical leftist Jiang Qing, and the military supremo began to show. Jiang Qing, unsurprisingly, felt that the PLA was a bastion of conservatism which was not showing sufficiently enthusiastic support for the young radicals. She wanted many of the top military men to be purged. But these were frequently supporters of Lin Biao, and the new Chief of Staff was a tough soldier called Huang Yongsheng, whom the Red Guards loathed because of the speed with which he had crushed some of their excesses.

In May Jiang Qing was promoted to number eight in the hierarchy, and Lin Biao was still number two. The summer of 1968 saw some of the worst violence of the Cultural Revolution. The Qinghua University campus was a battleground where many students died. Two main Red Guard factions (to which other Red Guard groups were affiliated) were known as the 'Heaven' and the 'Earth' factions. The Heaven faction was based on the Aeronautical Institute and was loyal to Zhou Enlai, and the Earth faction was based on the Geological Institute, was very radical and enjoyed the support of Jiang Qing and the leftist leaders.

Eventually even Mao realised that the violence had to come to an end, and at the end of July he called together the leaders of the Heaven and Earth factions. By all accounts it was a tearful meeting. Mao castigated the young leaders and told them that they had let him down. This was classic Mao Zedong. He had uttered calls to battle, and his instructions over the months had been a careful mass of contradictions. But now, when he saw that the country was in a state of anarchy, he found a scapegoat in the Red Guards who had merely been doing exactly what he had led them to believe he wanted done.

Mao himself now sent the Worker-Peasant Mao Zedong Thought Propaganda Teams into the universities to sort out the chaos. The arrival of the Work Team at Qinghua was accompanied by one of those bizarre additions so characteristic of the Cultural Revolution. To signal his blessing on their work Mao had given the team a present of mangoes. These had been a gift to Mao from a visiting Pakistani delegation. The fact that these mangoes had once belonged to Mao gave them an almost mystical significance. One of the mangoes was pickled and sent round the country by train to be gazed on with awe by the thousands who gathered to welcome the train. A factory even started to produce plastic mangoes.

The appearance of the Work Teams did not stop the violence, and some of the worst atrocities were committed as the 'ultra-leftists' were hunted out. Members of a group called the '16 May Group' were major targets. This group was something of an embarrassment. Although they were undeniably leftist, how could enthusiastic supporters of leftism be condemned out of hand? The solution was to label them 'ultra-rightists' and the 'black hand of Liu Shaoqi'. Many people were arrested and tortured to make them confess that they were members of the group. Finally the PLA were sent into many establishments to quell the excesses of the Work Teams. In Peking the elite Unit 8341, the 'Palace Guard', was sent to the Foreign Languages Institute on Mao's specific instruction after someone who worked there had alerted him to the state of affairs. Naturally, this boosted the power of the PLA.

In order to bring the Red Guards down to earth they were sent off in their millions to the countryside to 'learn from the peasants'. Schools were reopened but they were now to be run by workers and peasants, and there was a heavy emphasis on manual labour and studying Mao Zedong Thought. The Red Guards were not the only ones to go to the countryside.

Doctors were sent to rural clinics and hospitals. Cadres were sent to do stints in the May Seventh Cadre Schools, so called because on 7 May 1968 Mao had issued a declaration that all but the very highest-ranking cadres should regularly do a period of manual labour.

The universities reopened, but now entrance qualifications were based, not on academic achievement, but on political attitude. Preference would be given to students from a worker–peasant–soldier background, and no one would be considered unless he or she had spent at least a year working in the countryside, on the factory floor or in a military unit. Even then, unless the workers and peasants felt that the candidate showed the 'correct' attitude, he or she would still be ineligible.

University professors also had to take their turn either in the countryside or on the factory floor , and it was years before the universities were back to full student and staff strength. The intellectual waste was incalculable. The Chinese themselves say that they lost a decade of progress, and a generation of scientists and researchers, because of the Cultural Revolution. Most Chinese I have talked to condemn the Cultural Revolution and everything it stood for as one hundred per cent bad. But a tiny number are prepared to concede that some of Mao's aims were justified. They agree that a new elite had arisen, that there was a growing distance between the leaders and the led. Mao himself had always wanted to diminish the huge gap between town and countryside and mental and manual labour, and that was another of the aims of the Cultural Revolution. It had become increasingly difficult for children from worker or peasant background to get a tertiary education. Doctors were reluctant to work anywhere but the big cities. Urban children despised the peasantry.

When I first went to China in 1972 I had long discussions with Chinese about the whole question of manual labour, and why so many of them were appalled by the idea of having to do it. I pointed out that British students, myself included, had always done jobs during university vacations, and sometimes this involved back-breaking work such as picking potatoes (Mao would have approved of my own least-pleasant job – dealing with bedpans on a hospital ward), and that we chose to do this. It was clear that they thought that if we did not do such work then I was a liar, but if we did, then I was a fool. The expressions on their faces made it quite plain which they thought was worse. Whilst a voluntary job for a few weeks in the summer vacation is a far cry from being sent down to do years of labour in the often uncooperative earth of the Chinese countryside, I still felt some sympathy with Mao's view that the superior young urbanites needed to learn a greater appreciation of the peasants whose labour provided their food.

The peasants from whom the Red Guards were to learn the nobility of labour were often far from overjoyed by the influx. They regarded the urban teenagers as spoilt and useless. They were also extra mouths to feed, and the movement to send them to the countryside coincided with a leftist movement to do away with private plots and the raising of pigs, chickens and ducks. All these were vital to supplement the otherwise exceedingly meagre diet of the peasants. But now these were condemned as 'capitalist tails'. The resulting hunger did nothing to improve Red Guard–peasant relations. Furthermore, housing had to be found, and this was an added burden for the rural officials.

The experiment did, however, have some positive sides. A Chinese friend told me that she and a group of Red Guards were sent to a very backward area of Shaanxi Province. This was the same province of bare, brown loess hills in which the Communists had had their stronghold of Yanan. Even in the late 1960s the attitudes in the villages were very traditional. Initially the villagers were horrified by the easy camaraderie between the city boys and girls, and were particularly shocked that at the end of a day in the fields they would all sit around and wash their feet together, chatting. But gradually the young village girls got to know the Red Guard girls and heard their views on life, society and marriage. In time all the old traditions were undermined, as the village girls decided that they would no longer be subjected to the 'feudal' attitudes which had previously prevailed.

Although it was certainly a shameful waste of resources to send brilliant academics to hoe cabbages for years on end, for the most part those engaged in sensitive scientific research (such as nuclear research or rocketry) were spared. But a very gentle Professor of Metallurgy in Shanghai told me that he felt that his stint in a factory had done him good. He realised that much of his own work really *had* been too theoretical, and he enjoyed having to tackle the practical applications of his theories. Furthermore, he was appalled by the low technical level of many of the workers.

Although the system of 'barefoot doctors' started before the Cultural Revolution, it certainly gathered impetus during that period. These paramedics, with basic training in the diagnosis and treatment of common diseases, were an excellent solution to the problem of simple medical care in a country as huge and poor as China. When the Communists took power in 1949 they inherited a country where endemic disease was rife. Not only venereal disease and tuberculosis, but polio, meningitis, encephalitis and water-borne diseases like schistosomiasis were a terrible scourge. Through a well co-ordinated public health programme these were largely brought under control, and the Chinese are justly proud of the achievement. (Some of these diseases are once again on the upswing, and the reasons will be discussed in a later chapter.) The barefoot doctors were a part of their local community. They generally combined Western and Chinese medical techniques, and went a long way towards alleviating the general shortage of doctors.

With this mass migration to the countryside under way, in October 1968 the Central Committee held an enlarged Plenum presided over by Mao Zedong. This meeting formally expelled Liu Shaoqi from all his Party and state posts. This was totally unconstitutional, as the Party has no right to dismiss anyone from a *state* post. That can only be done by the National People's Congress, China's equivalent of a parliament. As a justification for this turning of Liu Shaoqi into a non-person (not that Mao ever felt the need to justify any of his actions) the meeting put forth a list of accusations against Liu. The major one was that he had been a KMT spy since the 1920s, and that he had surrendered to the KMT on three occasions and kept it a secret. He was accused of having married a US spy, Wang Guangmei, and it was stated that he had been diametrically opposed to Mao on a whole range of policy issues since the 1940s. Given the different backgrounds of the two men, their different experiences in the evolution of their Marxist views, and the fact that Liu had worked in the 'white' urban areas whilst Mao was working in the 'red' rural areas, it is natural that their approach to the path of Chinese socialism would differ. There is little evidence, however, that they were seriously at odds until the failure of the Great Leap Forward when Liu realised that Mao's views on mass mobili- sation as the way to speed up socialism had brought about disaster. But Mao brooked no opposition, and although he was prepared to forgive a man past mistakes if he then changed to a 'correct' way of thinking, if he did not, then not only his genuine mistakes but trumped up ones too would be used to discredit him completely. Liu Shaoqi died in custody in November 1969. He had been extremely ill and harshly treated. That, together with a lack of medical treatment and general deprivation, led to his death.

On 1 April 1969 the long-awaited Ninth Congress of the Central Committee took place. This was hailed as the culmi- nation of the Cultural Revolution and described as 'The Congress of Victory and Unity'. As events would shortly show, this was far from being the case. Lin Biao gave the main political report, and his position as Mao's successor was enshrined in the new Constitution. With the exception of Zhou Enlai, the Standing Committee of the Politburo was of a distinctly leftist persuasion – Mao, Lin Biao, Chen Boda and Kang Sheng. But now there was an interesting shift of allies. No sooner had Lin been named Mao's successor than it became clear that he and Chen Boda were drawing up battle lines against Mao and Zhou Enlai. The Ninth Central Com- mittee was a testament to the current power of the PLA. Over 60 per cent of its members were military men, a reflection of the same degree of military power in the newly formed Provincial Revolutionary Committees, as the new provincial governments were called. Military tribunals meted out 'people's justice', as the legal system was by then non- existent. Mao had instituted a mass movement on an Olym- pian scale, and the end result was that far from the masses being masters of their destiny, the PLA were the new czars of China – an interesting example of the enhanced power and importance of the military when China was in a state of social upheaval.

Immediately Mao set out to reduce the power of the military, and those with sensitive political antennae could see that he was already encompassing the downfall of the heir apparent. Mao travelled the country criticising Lin to the regional commanders. In photographs Lin was no longer at Mao's side, but behind him. Men who had been opposed to Lin were publicly reinstated.

As if further proof were needed, Lin's ally Chen Boda was disgraced at a crucial plenary session of the Central Committee held in August 1970 at the mountain resort of Lushan. Chen Boda was expelled from the Party and accused of ideological deviation. He was named 'the Chinese Trotsky' and a 'left Russian'. The real impetus behind this move is still largely obscure, but we do know that there were major clashes between Mao and Lin on both the domestic and foreign policy fronts.

Although foreign policy issues will be discussed in a later chapter, it is helpful to have a precis of China's changing foreign policy imperatives at that time. When the US intervened in Vietnam in 1965 the Chinese decided to give only indirect help to the Vietnamese, and so avoid direct confrontation with the US. With China's foreign relations in shreds as a result of the leftism of the Cultural Revolution, there was a complete reappraisal of the country's foreign policy. Relations with the Soviet Union were extremely tense in 1969, with a series of border clashes. The most famous was in March 1969 when troops from both sides clashed on Zhenbao Island in the Ussuri River, which divides the two countries in the northeast. It has often been said that China and the USSR were on the brink of war at that time. I think that this is probably an exaggeration, as there had been many previous skirmishes. But it almost certainly did concentrate Chinese minds on the importance of forming new alliances and a more equal dialogue even with those countries which had been subjected to abuse only two years before. The most important of these was the United States, and there is evidence that Lin Biao was totally opposed to any change of policy towards the US, whilst Mao and Zhou felt that the time had come for a major reappraisal of Sino-American relations, despite the fact that the Vietnam war was still raging.

Another source of contention was that Lin Biao and Chen Boda had apparently argued that the post of State Chairman should be reinstated. This was said to be a move on Lin's part to consolidate his own power, as he would have been the obvious candidate for the job. Mao was against the proposal, and was subsequently said to have seen this as a further sign of Lin's overweening ambition. Lin knew that time was not on his side, and decided to make a move before Mao moved against him. We shall probably never know the full truth of what is now known as 'The Lin Biao Affair', as it was months before the official Chinese version was made public, by which time the authorities had had time to think up a half-plausible tale. But even that version could still have been the product of one of the world's most imaginative thriller writers. It said that in September 1971 Lin Biao, having plotted several unsuccessful assassination attempts against Mao Zedong, panicked and fled the country in a Trident aeroplane. He was said to have been accompanied by his wife and son, and most of the high command. The plane crashed in Mongolia with the death of all on board.

CHAPTER FOUR

DEATH OF AN EMPEROR

The Lin Biao affair remains a mystery. Perhaps it always will. It was ten months before the Chinese gave out any details, and the first really full account was published in Taiwan. The Taiwanese version was so melodramatic that it was hard to credit, but analysis lent credence. The major piece of evidence of what was afoot was a document called the '571 Engineering Outline', said to be the policy document of Lin Biao and his allies. The Chinese for 571, *wuqiyi*, is a play on the characters meaning 'armed uprising', and that is clearly what Lin intended.

The document was an extraordinarily muddled production, with the ideas contained in it a strange mixture of conservatism and extreme leftism. But the main thread running through it was the need to get rid of Mao Zedong. Mao's nickname amongst the conspirators was B-52, because of his tendency to drop ideological bombs on the unsuspecting. Reading of the various methods with which Lin planned to get rid of Mao, one does not know whether to laugh at the madness of it all, or to weep over the incompetence. Lin had enormous military resources at his command, yet thought it necessary to work out six separate scenarios to encompass Mao's death. These ranged from blowing up the train in which he would be travelling to attacking it with flame-throwers and bazookas. Lin and his allies were spurred on to make their attempt on Mao because of dark hints which he had dropped in the summer of 1971 that he knew something was afoot. He then went off on an inspection tour of the two military regions which just might have been prepared to support Lin, Nanjing

(Nanking) and Canton (Guangzhou). It was whilst he was on this tour that he was to be eliminated.

What followed was a tale quite Shakespearian in its mixture of would-be assassins who lose their nerve and rely on their wives to get them out of a fix, botched attacks and a final scenario in which all the unrighteous perish whilst the upright survive. Put more prosaically, when Lin realised that the assassination attempt, masterminded by Lin's son, a high-ranking air force officer, had gone wrong, he panicked. He ordered an air force Trident jet to be made ready for him, but this unusual demand was relayed to the ever-watchful Zhou Enlai. The Trident took off, but later crashed in Mongolia, with the death of all on board.

There are still more questions unanswered than answered in this extraordinary affair. Initially, reports from Peking said that as well as Lin, his wife, his son and various aides, the Chief of Staff and three other very high-ranking military men, who were also members of the Politburo, were fellow passengers. Even at the time this seemed improbable, and all doubts were confirmed when the four in question turned up as co-defendants at the trial of the Gang of Four in 1980. They had clearly been in prison without trial for the preceding decade. It was said that the plane crashed because of lack of fuel. Although the botched coup, if that is what it was, shows that the Lins, father and son, were no master conspirators, it is unlikely that they would have taken off in a plane which had not been refuelled. There are two possible answers. One is that Zhou Enlai had made sure that it was short of fuel, and the other is that the Trident was shot down by a Chinese missile.

I think that the latter is the more likely explanation. It was embarrassing enough that the event should have happened at all, and that the plane should have crashed in Mongolia. But if Lin really was heading for Moscow, as it is claimed, the prospect of his being given a hero's welcome by the Russians would have been most embarrassing to Peking. However, it is likely that a number of the Soviet leaders would have found Lin Biao's arrival a distinct nuisance, as by then the tensions of 1969 had slightly lessened.

Doubts have always been expressed as to whether Lin, always so anti-Soviet, would have fled to the lair of the arch-revisionists. But since there is evidence that Lin was unhappy with the growing rapprochement with the United States, it is possible that he had a change of heart. After all, it was in April 1971 that an American ping-pong team visited Peking, marking a completely new phase in Sino-American relations. Then in July Henry Kissinger made his secret visit to Peking to prepare for President Nixon's historic visit in February 1972.

Perhaps the most important question of all is, was Lin Biao really on the plane at all? The Chinese have produced evidence that he was, but it is less than convincing. The whole truth may never come out, but whether it does or not, the important thing is that the Chinese people and the rest of the world were told that Mao's chosen successor had committed an act of dastardly betrayal.

The result was that, although the PLA had remained loyal to Mao, he was determined that there should be a shake-up in the armed forces. They had been such a vital element in restoring order after the violence of the Cultural Revolution that they now permeated every sector of society, and Mao intended to lessen their power. Now, instead of the whole country being called on to 'learn from the PLA', the PLA was called on 'to learn from the whole country'. Once again Mao stressed that although power grows out of the barrel of a gun, 'the Party must always control the gun'.

Party rebuilding in the provinces had started in late 1970, and was completed nine months later. This also helped to reduce the concentrated power of the PLA. Mao's native province of Hunan was the first to set up the new Provincial Party Committee, with one Hua Guofeng as its head. In late 1971 Hua moved to Peking, apparently to help with the investigation of senior cadres. This previously obscure figure, who within a few years was to be the leader of China, was born in Shanxi Province, but began to make his mark in Hunan. Physically, he was rather like Mao, but there the resemblance ended. He was a plodding, uncharismatic character, and it is not easy to work out exactly where he stood on the political spectrum. However, if one looks at his speeches and the policies he supported, it is fair to say that he was closer to the Gang of Four than to the pragmatic policies of Deng Xiaoping. He was also a most loyal supporter of Mao Zedong.

Policies now see-sawed up and down. In mid-1970 students were readmitted to Peking and Qinghua Universities for the first time since 1966. Understandably, given the lengthy gap, thousands of potential students were eager for a place, and admission was by examination. However, preference was given to those from a worker–peasant background, and every candidate had to state his or her class background on the application forms. Those whose parents were in political disgrace were unlikely to get a place. The old Chinese tradition of guilt by blood was once again to the fore.

Very soon educators clashed over the policy on education. The combination of a long gap in education and the fact that most of the new students came from proletarian backgrounds, meant that many of them were not up to standard. I arrived in Peking in October 1972 to work in the British Embassy and on my first trip to Peking University heard the lament that many of the new entrants only had the educational level of a fourteen-year-old. There was a certain irony in this, as the man who complained was the well-known physicist, Zhou Peiyuan. Yet at the beginning of the Cultural Revolution Zhou had been one of the most vociferous critics of the then President of Peking University, Lu Ping. As I mentioned in the previous chapter, Lu Ping was accused of putting too much emphasis on academic qualifications, to the neglect of politics and manual labour. Now it was Zhou's turn to regret the current emphasis on practical learning, and the fact that the new physics students needed a crash course in maths before they could start their studies.

But people like Zhou Peiyuan were having to combat a rearguard action from the leftists, who condemned the increasing emphasis on academic achievement and examinations. What was wrong with students taking books into exams, and asking each other the answers, they asked? Schoolchildren and students who simply handed in blank exam. papers, or criticised the need for exams at all, were praised in the Chinese press. The curriculum for primary and secondary schools was extremely restricted. Whenever I visited a school at that time, I was appalled by the high content of Marxism–Leninism–Mao Zedong Thought, and by the lack of much else. All subjects were taught from a political viewpoint, and it always struck me as a little irrelevant to teach children such English sentences as 'Full of love for Chairman Mao, the peasant plants the rice seedlings'. The children chanted all their lessons in unison, yet could not answer even the simplest question if addressed to any of them individually. There was a heavy emphasis on manual labour and many schools had their own basic workshops, in which the children either made simple products or packaged goods which were then sold to raise money for the school to buy equipment.

I arrived in Peking shortly after Britain and China had established relations at full ambassadorial level, and just before the visit to Peking by the then British Foreign Secretary, Sir Alec Douglas-Home. This was the first visit by a British Foreign Secretary, and was a further sign of the increasing normalisation of China's foreign relations. Yet my first impression was of a country which was holding its breath, completely unsure of what might happen next. People went steadily about their business and said as little as possible about anything even mildly sensitive.

A daily reading of the *People's Daily* was a good indication of the unsettled nature of current policies. One day there would be an article on the importance of stepping up agricultural and industrial output, and the next an article saying that just because production was to be increased this did not mean that production was all-important or that class struggle had come to an end. Peasants were allowed to have private plots again, but there was a great debate as to how many pigs should be privately owned. One? Two? More? When did a pig cease to be a legitimate means of supporting a peasant family and become instead a symbol of heterodoxy? Small wonder that most Chinese were in a state of permanent nervous confusion.

But for a foreigner living in China it was a fascinating period. For a start there were very few of us, initially only about 1500 in the diplomatic community. Added to these were a few journalists and a handful of businessmen. One became very proprietorial about the country, and most disapproving of the ever-increasing number of tourists!

What made it so interesting was that trying to understand China was something that one did *despite* the Chinese. Ordinary Chinese were far too afraid to talk to foreigners, and our only contacts were with officials, mainly from the Foreign Ministry. However, those with whom we had the closest dealings were wholly admirable people, and my friendship with them has lasted until today. They were treading a very fine line in their dealings with us, but it was a great pleasure to have them to dinner and to discuss a variety of subjects, ranging from Chinese politics (dangerous) to Jane Austen (slightly less so).

So our analysis was based on the evidence of our own eyes and ears, and the ideas which we bounced off each other. A number of diplomats of various nationalities spoke Chinese and whilst we undoubtedly formed a very incestuous clique, we were often correct in our assessments of what was going on. For instance, there was a heated poster campaign in 1973. Since it was a hot and uncomfortable job standing in the sun reading the lengthy posters, the junior diplomats took it in turns to go each day to look at them. It was quite clear from these posters that all the old enmities of the Cultural Revolution were still very much to the fore. Factory workers came from all over the country to put up posters complaining about the situation in their factories. Depending on the writer's own political leanings one learnt either that there was leftist disruption in the factories, or that the management was 'putting production in command'. There were accusations of corruption and victimisation. It was clear that the situation was extremely tense.

In those early days many visitors to China, and especially to Peking, complained about its drabness, and the fact that everyone wore the same sexless blue, grey or olive green. But I loved it. I arrived in the autumn when the skies are the clearest blue and are a wonderful contrast to the dun-coloured earth of the North China Plain. When the trees shed their leaves in Peking one could see the traditional grey houses with their overlapping grey slate roofs. Then followed the winter, very cold, but bone dry and with the same clear blue skies. The lakes froze over so deeply that we could safely skate on them. One of the loveliest sights in the world is a winter sun setting over the lake at the Summer Palace, with maybe one lone cyclist wheeling his bike over the ice in the golden haze of sunset.

Although we were very restricted in our movements at that

time, we were allowed to go to the Great Wall and the Ming
tombs, and I never tired of the latter. The tombs, where the
Emperors of the Ming dynasty were buried, fell into increasing disrepair, but after the endless crowds of Peking there was
nothing more peaceful than an afternoon at the tombs,
surrounded by jagged mountains and cypress trees. In the
summer the trees provided shade, and in the autumn, after
the leaves had fallen, the branches of the persimmon trees
glowed with golden fruit. It was one of the few peaceful places
in or around Peking.

For both Chinese and foreigners living in China in the early
and mid-1970s, the country was a cultural wasteland. One of
the greatest ironies of the so-called Cultural Revolution was
its destruction of so many facets of Chinese culture. The few
novels and short stories available were about heroic commune
leaders or army men, and the style in which they were written
was extremely simple and used a minimal number of Chinese
characters. The heroes and heroines were all created in the
best socialist tradition — self-sacrificing, hard-working and
incorruptible. The individual was of no importance, only the
society in which the individual existed. What we individualis-
tic Westerners found particularly unacceptable was that both
in fiction and in real life so many priorities seemed to have
been stood on their heads. State property counted for more
than people, and one frequently read extravagant praise for a
hero who had sacrificed himself to save state property. The
property in question might have been a couple of telegraph
poles about to fall into a river or a horse about to be run over
by a truck. In each case the property was saved and the man
died. Somehow one could not have much faith in a government which placed telegraph poles and horses above human
life.

Apart from the paucity of literature, opera, plays and films
were also set in a socialist concrete of Jiang Qing's making.
There were about eight 'model' operas, plays and ballets,
which we saw *ad nauseam*, for want of an alternative. Jiang
Qing had accomplished what she set out to do in transforming
Chinese opera, and in many ways those ancient operatic
traditions of the battle between good and evil were an ideal
vehicle for the current Communist battle between socialist
and revisionist. The characters were either black or white,

with no shades of grey. The heroes were members of the PLA, workers or peasants. The villains were the KMT, class enemies, wicked landlords, the Japanese or the United Nations troops in Korea. Jiang Qing supervised every last detail of the operas, even down to the pompoms on the ballet shoes. Some of the works, such as *The White-Haired Girl* were genuinely moving tales of oppression, although that story predated Jiang Qing's cultural take-over. But I found it hard to take seriously ballets like *The Red Detachment of Women*, although they were actually no more improbable than many Western ballets. The problem was that the cultural field had been so battered during the 1960s that anyone connected with it was terrified of creating a work which would then come under attack, so a frightful sterility set in. Mao's own guidelines on literature and art had been characteristically vague, and writers and artists scarcely knew how to evaluate them.

Local opera, as opposed to the more rarefied Peking opera, enjoyed a revival. Every region in China has its own operatic tradition, and creates its own opera using local dialect. These operas are usually much more colourful and lively than Peking opera, and I remember seeing a marvellous performance in the south-western Province of Sichuan in 1974 which was very funny and optimistic. The hero got the girl, and there was not a single atom of class-consciousness in the whole opera.

Although there were major problems in assessing China's artistic tradition, the one area in which the Chinese made major strides during the Cultural Revolution was archaeology. This area of research was less ideologically fraught, as so many of the artefacts were made by skilled artisans rather than by the elite, so their evaluation and preservation posed less of a dilemma. One of the greatest archaeological finds of modern times, the Terracotta Army at Xi'an, was first discovered in the early 1970s, and the great Chinese Archaeological Finds exhibition was held in London during the winter of 1973.

As in every other aspect of China at that time, there were also anomalies in the cultural field. 1973 was a halcyon year for music lovers. There were visits from three Western orchestras – the London Philharmonic, the Vienna and the Philadelphia. These were the first performances of Western music for years, and much skulduggery was afoot to get hold of one of the precious tickets. It was deeply moving to see the emotion of those who were able to attend the performances, especially as they were often people from fields that had been hardest hit by the Cultural Revolution. But the musical pleasure was short-lived. Scarcely were the orchestral visits over than an attack was launched on Western music, and Beethoven and Schubert were castigated as 'bourgeois'. This was an example of the 'struggle between two lines' which was going on in every field.

Deng Xiaoping had returned to centre stage in April 1973 as a Vice-Premier, and he was soon followed by a number of fellow 'capitalist-roaders'. This caused much contention amongst the leadership, as the role of Deng and like-minded leaders was to get China back on the road to agricultural and industrial production, whilst the leftist leaders felt that this would lead to a negation of everything for which the Cultural Revolution had been launched. It seemed that a bargain had been struck between the leftists and the moderates. Deng could not have returned without Mao Zedong's sanction, but having agreed to his return, Mao never gave the least outward support either to Zhou Enlai or to Deng.

In August 1973 the Chinese Communist Party held its Tenth Congress, and it is probably correct to say that this congress, rather than the 1969 Ninth Congress, marked the end of the Cultural Revolution. It was at this meeting that all the crimes of Lin Biao were laid before a disbelieving public. As Liu Shaoqi's name had been thoroughly blackened in 1968, so now in 1973 it was Lin Biao's turn. Lin, the great military strategist was now designated a coward and a fool who would have lost every battle had not Mao saved the situation. His treachery, like that of Liu, was also traced back to the 1920s. As with Liu, no one believed a word of it, and now Lin's reputation as a military strategist has been restored.

The succession of men who have apparently betrayed Mao is a source of deep embarrassment. In each case it was said that Mao had, of course, known for years that the person in question was a scoundrel and a traitor, but that is simply not credible. Would Mao have committed an act of such extraordinary foolhardiness as to name a man as his successor merely to flush him out from his lair? Even Mao's Machiavellian nature would not need to carry matters to such lengths. And if Mao was such a poor judge of the men whom he considered to be worthy successors, then what does this say for his judgement in other areas? The panache with which the Chinese leadership rewrites the past is always breathtaking, and has its roots in history. Each dynasty rewrote the history of the preceding dynasty to the successor's best advantage. But the complete distortion of the truth which has been so characteristic of Chinese politics since 1949 raises interesting questions. Do the Chinese leaders so despise their people that they feel free to feed them any farrago of lies? Or do they fully understand that people will not believe a word of the latest historical gloss but, being Chinese, would not dream of being so ill-bred as to openly challenge the lies? Whatever the answer, it has allowed China's leaders to get away with a great deal.

The Tenth Party Congress could be seen as a truce between the warring factions, but it was clearly an uneasy truce. This time no one was nominated as a successor to Mao, and the leadership was now to be a mixture of old, middle-aged and young. But the real surprise was the meteoric rise of the dashing young Shanghai radical, Wang Hongwen. Wang was made second Vice-Chairman of the Party, and delivered the Party work report. His report still indicated a commitment to radical policies, and was quite different in tone from Zhou Enlai's more measured report. Wang was photographed at Mao's side, and people began to wonder whether this was the new heir apparent to the Party throne. Along with more moderate souls, all of the Shanghai radicals (alias the Shanghai Mafia) remained in the Politburo. Their policies remained as leftist as ever, and as they controlled the media they had the power to propagate that message. It was not a recipe for smooth government. And indeed, the target of the next attack was Zhou Enlai himself.

One has always needed good detective qualities to pinpoint the victims of press campaigns in China, and the 1973 and 1974 campaign to criticise Confucius was one of the most recondite that I can remember. At the same time there was a massive academic reassessment of Confucianism and Legalism. Briefly, Confucius was a philosopher–sage who lived some 500 years before Christ, and wandered around China offering advice to rulers on the best way to govern their subjects. He preached the view that each man had his place in society, and there could never be complete equality, even between brothers, as the younger must always defer to the elder. Confucius believed in benevolent rule and the status quo. At that time China was still a slave society.

The Legalists, on the other hand, were a much harsher breed. They came to the fore in the third century B.C., at the time of the first Emperor of the Qin Dynasty. Qin Shi Huangdi was a despot who unified all China, built the Great Wall and imposed a series of reforms on a feudal society, with much death and destruction in the process. The Legalists believed that man could only be controlled by harsh laws. The radicals of the 1970s favoured the Legalists because they were seen as progressive, because they advocated struggle, and because they believed that laws rather than faith in the inherent goodness of human nature would bring about social evolution. (There is a certain irony in this, as in the 1970s what laws there were in China were constantly flouted by the authorities.) Confucianism, on the other hand, was seen as retrogressive.

A sinister note crept into the campaign with a very specific attack on 'The Duke of Zhou'. The Duke in question was traditionally considered to be the embodiment of all the Confucian virtues, and in 1974 was used as a symbol of elitism and conservatism. I remember being completely taken aback when I first read the criticism of the Duke of Zhou, because it could only have been an attack on Zhou Enlai. The idea that the Chinese press would openly attack the Prime Minister was almost inconceivable, and was proof of the leftists' control of the media.

Shortly afterwards there was an even more bizarre twist to the campaign. No longer was the Duke of Zhou the villain, but Lin Biao. The moderates were counter-attacking, and the campaign to 'Criticise Lin Biao and Confucius' lasted until November 1974. Lin was now attacked for 'idealism', but the linking of Lin with Confucius strained the imagination even more than the almost overt attack on Zhou Enlai.

In May 1974 Zhou Enlai went into hospital, by now gravely ill with cancer, and from that time until his death in January 1976 Deng Xiaoping acted as unofficial Prime Minister. The long-awaited Fourth National People's Congress took place in January 1975, the first new congress for eleven years. The revised state Constitution reflected the 1954 Constitution, and indicated a new economic pragmatism, respect for lawful government and the individual's right to work for himself. Again there was an attempt at compromise. Although Deng Xiaoping was now Vice-Chairman of the Party as well as Vice-Premier of the State Council, he was also appointed Chief of Staff of the Army; the radical Zhang Chunqiao was appointed Head of the PLA's General Political Department (a very sensitive job, and one which had brought about the downfall of many of its incumbents).

Mao showed his complete contempt for this spirit of pragmatism by not attending the congress. He made sure, however, that everyone knew that he was not absent through illness by receiving the German politician Franz Josef Strauss in the eastern city of Hangzhou whilst the congress was taking place. Mao's disapproval seemed to put the kiss of death on any hopes of unity. The new Constitution had, for the first time, enshrined the right to strike, and soon Hangzhou was paralysed by strikes. Finally, large numbers of soldiers had to be sent in to quell the disorder.

Towards the end of 1975 the polemics against Deng Xiaoping grew fiercer, and wall posters attacked him for emphasising production. He was accused of relying too much on imported foreign plant whilst ignoring class struggle. As dyed-in-the-wool Marxists, Deng's critics argued that you cannot import capitalist technology without importing a bit of capitalist organisation. But the accusations were in the radical-controlled press, and were not a sign of a genuine mass movement against Deng. Throughout the year more and more people who had been ousted in the Cultural Revolution were being rehabilitated, to the chagrin of the leftists, and it was clear that serious battle lines were again being drawn up.

The armed forces were an uncertain element in the equation. There had been a major shake-up in the military regions in the autumn of 1973, and a regional commander known to be loyal to Mao was moved to command the Nanjing military region, which included the vitally important Shanghai garrison. A yet more sinister development occurred in 1974 when it was disclosed that a new 'armed defence group' had been set up in Shanghai to maintain law and order. This group was to be completely outside the control of the army, and would be armed with sophisticated weapons. Shanghai was turning into a city state, and only Mao would have had the power to make such critical innovations. Although there is no hard evidence, it is possible that Mao, believing that China was once again slipping into revisionism, was prepared to launch another leftist movement out of Shanghai, aided and abetted by the Gang of Four.

The Chinese always say that the Year of the Dragon brings an extraordinary mixture of bad and good, and 1976 was a Dragon Year in which the good stayed stubbornly in the background until the last months of the year. Zhou Enlai died on 6 January, and although it was still the end of the previous lunar year it was a bad portent. The nation was plunged into genuine mourning, for Zhou was much loved. Deng Xiaoping read the eulogy, but Mao Zedong did not even attend the obsequies for the man who had been his most loyal ally for forty years. Mao ignored Zhou's wish that Deng Xiaoping should succeed him as Premier, and instead appointed the colourless Hua Guofeng as Acting Premier. Mao also, quite unconstitutionally, appointed Hua a Vice-Chairman of the Party. However, it is probably true that whilst the leftists would have resisted Deng Xiaoping's appointment as Premier, the moderates were prepared to accept Hua as a compromise candidate.

The Gang of Four knew that there would be a tremendous outburst of sentiment on the day when Zhou Enlai's remains were removed to the cemetery for revolutionary heroes at Babaoshan, and so kept the date quiet. But in China things can rarely be kept secret. On 11 January millions lined the route to the cemetery, and the entire country shared their grief. Zhou had very wisely decreed that he was to be cremated and his ashes were to be scattered. After all, one cannot desecrate scattered ashes, nor can they become a focus for political ferment. But for three days they were placed in the Workers' Cultural Palace, to the east of the Tiananmen in the centre of Peking, and after paying their respects, thousands of people then crossed over to the Martyrs' Monument in Tiananmen Square, the setting for so many crucial events in Chinese history, and added their white flowers of mourning to those already there. People recited their own poems, many of which were politically very sensitive. These quite spontaneous actions were a deliberate snub to the leftists, and they knew it.

With Zhou's death congratulatory messages flowed in from the provinces to the new Acting Premier. Everyone hailed his appointment, although scarcely anyone knew anything about him. Meanwhile, Deng Xiaoping had not been seen since he delivered the eulogy at Zhou Enlai's funeral. It was quite clear to everyone that another political struggle was taking place. The Year of the Dragon foretold the coming drama with a shower of meteorites in the north-east.

The Qingming Festival is the time when people sweep their ancestors' graves and mourn the dead. As the day approached at the beginning of April, large numbers of wreaths to commemorate Zhou Enlai began to appear around the Martyrs' Monument in Tiananmen Square. This was a clear challenge to the authority of the Gang of Four. Poems of extraordinary boldness were attached to the wreaths. Many lamented the death of Zhou Enlai, but many were openly critical of Jiang Qing and her allies. This outburst was an expression of grief, but it was also a declaration of war.

Overnight on 4 April the wreaths were taken away, and as the news spread through the city there was a great sense of outrage. On the next day thousands flocked to Tiananmen Square, and the situation was orderly until the security police ordered people to leave. Then the violence started. Vehicles were overturned and burnt and the security headquarters attacked. The Mayor of Peking, Wu De, arrived and told people to leave. When they did not go the militia moved in, and the confrontation was brutal. A large number of people were arrested and beaten. People were appalled to see an attack on the masses by the masses, for the militia was largely composed of factory workers.

The Tiananmen Incident, as it came to be known, was declared a counter-revolutionary movement and blamed on Deng Xiaoping, ironic in the light of events in Tiananmen Square in the summer of 1989. Once again he was dismissed from all his posts. A campaign was launched against him in the press and this was clearly not a mass campaign, but one orchestrated by a minority of leftist leaders. In July the

Dragon struck again with the death of the much-loved old revolutionary, Zhu De, and this fuelled everyone's fears that the old order was passing, and that the new order could be infinitely worse.

Then the Tangshan earthquake struck north-east China. During that period China would not accept foreign help for natural disasters, so it is doubtful whether many people had any idea of the magnitude of that earthquake. It completely flattened the industrial city of Tangshan, killing over a quarter of a million people and badly injuring another quarter of a million. The 1988 earthquake in Armenia, tragic though it was, was nothing in comparison with Tangshan. Although seismologists around the world knew that there had been a serious earthquake, and that its tremors had struck Peking, it was a long time before the full details came out. It was known that the PLA had immediately been mobilised and that they did an excellent job. But the cost in human life and material resources was colossal, and occupied Hua Guofeng and his colleagues throughout the next weeks. In Peking buildings were so badly damaged that people had to camp out in hastily constructed mud huts, with plastic sheeting to keep out the summer rain, and thousands continued to live in them throughout the cold northern winter of 1976–77. Once again the Dragon had lashed its tail.

Then came the final blow. On 9 September Mao Zedong died. The Chinese were devastated. Despite all the catastrophes which he had visited upon them, he had been their liberator, their guide and mentor, their god, the 'Red Sun in our Hearts' for over three decades. Mixed with real grief was also a sense of great apprehension. For who could ever take his place?

Before looking at the next dramatic development, it is necessary to try to evaluate the roles played by Zhou Enlai and Mao Zedong, the two men who did so much for China over so long a period. It will probably be many years before the good and the bad will be more objectively weighed in the balance, and there may always be a larger question mark over the enigmatic Zhou Enlai than over Mao.The Chinese themselves are trying to analyse the role which Zhou played over the decades, and his relationship with Mao. There was a major conference on Zhou in Tianjin (Tientsin) in the autumn of

1988, and it was more of a canonisation than a truly objective analysis. For the past decade surprisingly little has been said officially about Zhou, and it appears that the Party was still cautiously assessing his role. Now, however, they seem to have concluded that he was even more praiseworthy than Mao.

How Chinese evaluate Zhou Enlai depends to a large extent on the age of the evaluator. The middle-aged and old still have the deepest respect and admiration for him. They see him as one of the founding fathers of the People's Republic, the loyal disciple of Mao, the man to whom anyone could turn to demand that an injustice be righted. Because so many people in the bureaucracy were paralysed by the uncertainties of the times, sometimes even the most trivial decisions were referred up to Zhou Enlai. One even heard tales of factories writing to the Premier to plead for help if they found it impossible to get vital raw materials. So the Premier of the world's most populous country wasted valuable time making decisions that a clerk should have made.

Zhou Enlai's charm and diplomacy were legendary, and made all those who met him or knew anything about him disinclined to believe anything but good of him. There is also not a shadow of doubt that he had great personal courage. This was particularly evident in the Cultural Revolution when he had to face both direct harassment by Red Guards and the more insidious attacks of the leftists. At some risk to himself he intervened on behalf of other leaders who were being persecuted. But still we have to ask the awkward question, why was he so unswervingly loyal to Mao? Why did he do nothing to mitigate Mao's increasingly erratic behaviour? Again, the answer depends on the age of the Chinese with whom one discusses this. The older ones argue that he had no choice. If he had stood up to Mao and condemned the Cultural Revolution he would have been ousted in the same way as Liu Shaoqi, Deng Xiaoping and other dissenting voices. By going along with the Cultural Revolution he was able to work behind the scenes to soften the worst excesses and to save some of those under attack. Then, when the madness had passed, Zhou was still there to help a stricken China to slowly gather itself together. This interpretation depicts Zhou as the type of Chinese administrator who will sacrifice even his peace of mind for the good of the state.

The young do not all see it in the same light. They argue that Zhou should have had the moral fibre of Liu Shaoqi and Peng Dehuai, and opposed Mao and all his works. If he had perished in the attempt, as they did, so be it. They see him as a man who was so determined to keep his position that he supported Mao in policies that must have offended every fibre in his body. They remember that Zhou also waved the *Little Red Book* during the Cultural Revolution (though one has to admit that he always looked rather sheepish as he did so), and never seemed to oppose anything that Mao decreed. Yes, he saved some people in the Cultural Revolution, but if he had taken a firmer stand he might have been able to prevent the excesses. They point to the other kind of classical Chinese administrator – the one who died for his principles.

Since Zhou was far too careful a politician ever to voice his own views too frankly in public, we may never be able to assess his motivations or his principles. There is no doubt that his own political instincts were diametrically opposed to Mao's. Mao always inclined sharply towards the Left, Zhou saw leftism as a major threat to China. Mao gloried in China's poverty, Zhou saw it as something on which an all-out attack should be launched. Mao despised and disliked intellectuals, whilst Zhou saw them as vital to the country's development. So for forty years Zhou was the most loyal minister of a man who was in every respect the complete opposite of himself. The reason for such loyalty may have been because Zhou, who was a convinced Communist, saw in Mao the only man who had the strength and ruthlessness to hold China together and push it forward. And when Zhou saw the destruction that Mao caused in his declining years he believed that it was his duty to try to salvage what he could of the wreckage.

Assessing Mao Zedong and his legacy is both easier and more difficult. It is easier in the sense that Mao's actions and the events they precipitated are so well known, and more difficult because the horrors for which he was responsible in his latter years are in danger of blinding us to his achievements. I have not the slightest doubt that only Mao Zedong had the determination and the ruthlessness to drag his country and his people out of the morass of warlordism, foreign oppression and backwardness in which they were mired. Mao's own unshakeable belief that he was right and would eventually be proved to be right helped him to withstand every assault, and to battle on through conditions and circumstances which would have destroyed a lesser mortal. But the question then is, would it have been better if Mao had died or been ousted almost immediately after the establishment of the People's Republic? Is a man who is the perfect leader in times of war also the right man in times of peace?

One could argue that without Mao's bold vision the move towards co-operative farming would have taken much longer. That is true, but as China has now reverted to individual farming, was the whole co-operative and commune movement not a complete waste of time, effort and lives? The eminent Party historian, Liao Gailong, told me earlier this year that the Party's assessment of the commune system was that it was wholly negative, but I must take issue with this view. With the exception of the disastrous famine years during the Great Leap Forward, there was certainly greater agricultural output than before. One must treat with caution the claims by China's present leaders that until the economic reforms were started in 1978, China's agricultural development had been disastrous. Figures do not support this view. Even during the Cultural Revolution, when one might have expected truly appalling figures, grain output rose from 210 million tons in 1965 to 240 in 1970. It is true that when the reforms were started grain production shot up very rapidly but, as will be discussed in the next chapter, grain production has run into considerable trouble over the past four years, precisely because of the present reforms.

The official Chinese assessment is that Mao's legacy was 70 per cent good and 30 per cent bad. It is only natural that the leadership should give Mao a higher rating for good than many of the population would. Many of the current leaders were themselves very close to Mao for much of his life, and in wholly condemning Mao they would also be questioning their own legitimacy. What Mao did was to create a constant climate of uncertainty, and even fear. The endless campaigns meant that no policy was given time to consolidate its gains. Because of Mao's visceral loathing of intellectuals (whilst being himself something of a scholar) the great intellectual resources of the country were scandalously wasted. People were afraid to speak out in opposition because they saw what the consequences were for those who did. Mao's own ideological pronouncements were often so vague that people either did not know what he really meant, or the less scrupulous twisted them to mean whatever suited them best. Mao was very good at criticising what he abhorred, but much less good at suggesting clear philosophies to take their place. He used catch-all phrases to attack his enemies, and any epithet could be attached to any victim. He slowly destroyed the faith of millions who had trusted him and the Party, and left them with nothing to fill the chasm of ruined hopes. The man who filled millions of Chinese with optimism and a willingness to make great sacrifices betrayed their trust so often that his legacy is one of cynicism. The man who talked so much about 'the masses' created a situation in which eventually the individual could only rely on himself, and to hell with society.

People in developed countries make a mistake in assuming that the people of developing countries are indifferent to such matters as free speech and democracy. Even in the most repressed of societies people are beginning boldly to demand free speech and democracy as a right, and not a privilege graciously bestowed by the leadership. It is often argued that in developing countries people only care about having enough to eat, and it is quite true that for vast numbers in China that has always been a prime concern. But as recent events have shown this has been changing rapidly over the past decade in China, and will be discussed in the next chapter. If we grant that Mao Zedong's legacy on human rights did him no credit, (although, ironically, a number of Chinese are beginning to view Mao's record more leniently following Deng Xiaoping's brutal suppression of the pro-democracy demonstrations in June 1989), what about his legacy in ameliorating the physical hardships of his people?

There he fared better. He took over a country which was very poor, and in which famine was common; the great rivers flooded their banks year after year killing thousands, and endemic diseases took a terrible toll. When he died the food problem had basically been solved (leaving aside the terrible famine of the Great Leap era). People might have been poor, and indeed were, but there were not the hordes of beggars that one sees in India. Endemic diseases were largely under control. The huge and turbulent rivers had been tamed. The vast majority of children could expect to get at least a primary education.

Mao himself would probably have said that such successes were enough for him. He would have scorned the importance of a truly democratic society, ridiculed the notion that human beings need peace and stability. Although he saw all about him the frailty of human nature, he still held ruthlessly to the ideal that man can be constantly forged in the fire of revolution, and finally emerge as a shining 'proletarian tool'. Towards the end of his life Mao was certainly suffering from senility, and was emotional and somewhat unpredictable. Someone close to Mao told me that in the early 1970s, as old revolutionaries were rehabilitated following the Cultural Revolution, Mao would embrace them with tears on his cheeks, and express his joy that they had returned. And yet Mao had frequently been responsible for their earlier disgrace! My informant remarked caustically that such emotionalism is particularly dangerous in a one-man dictatorship.

When Mao died the major and immediate concern was, who was to succeed him? Hua Guofeng was the front runner. Immediately a campaign was started to shore up Hua's legitimacy. Since the majority of the population knew nothing about him, lengthy biographies were circulated in the press. Characteristically for that period, Hua was not simply depicted as an able leader. Instead the hagiography described a man of almost superhuman qualities. He had performed miracles in agricultural innovation whilst governing Hunan Province. He had only to spend a few moments addressing a problem, and it was solved. He worked night and day for the good of the people. And, above all, Mao had anointed him as his successor with the words 'With you in charge, I am at ease.' No one was convinced. It was unclear when Mao had made such a statement, and he could have been referring to some quite different task which he had entrusted to Hua. And indeed, a very well-informed source in Peking told me that the task in question had been the management of the anti-Deng Xiaoping campaign which was under way in the provinces in the months before Mao's death. But Hua had to establish his legitimacy, and he knew that vast numbers of the population would ask themselves what right he had to assume the mantle of the 'Great Teacher'. Astonishingly, for a short while Hua was, in formal terms, the most powerful leader Communist China has known. He was simultaneously Party Chairman, Prime Minister, and he had also inherited Mao's key role as head of the Party's Military Commission. But Hua knew that other leaders would be waiting in the wings, ready to snatch his victory from him.

On 1 October 1976, China's National Day, there was a great show of unity amongst the leadership, and Jiang Qing made a positive speech about the importance of everybody working together. Never were appearances more deceptive. On 6 October the State Council Guard Unit 8341, the 'Palace Guard', arrested the Gang of Four – Jiang Qing, Zhang Chunqiao, Yao Wenyuan and Wang Hongwen – and some of their close supporters. The whole country (except for the supporters of the Gang of Four) let out the collective breath it had been holding for years. There were such celebrations that there was hardly a bottle of alcohol left on the shelves. People in Shanghai told me that cyclists crashed into each other without coming to blows, and a favourite dish in the ensuing days was a dish of crabs – one female and three males. With their sideways approach and their vicious claws, crabs were said to typify the members of the Gang of Four.

Now followed one of the most vicious campaigns that China has ever seen. This was not a campaign of violence, but of total character assassination. Articles, cartoons and poems were used to attack the Gang of Four. It is true that many atrocities must be laid at the door of the Gang of Four, but they were also used as scapegoats because no one had quite enough courage to lay the blame for the years of horror at the door of the real culprit – Mao Zedong. All four members of the Gang were savagely criticised, but there was a degree of sexism in the attacks on Jiang Qing which was extremely distasteful. Every scurrilous tale was dug up and publicised. She was accused of having had a stream of lovers, and of having manipulated Mao Zedong. She was likened to the fearsome Empress Wu Zetian of the Tang Dynasty. Now the Empress Wu was a ruthless woman who had no hesitation in cruelly murdering her enemies and rivals, but she was certainly no worse than many Chinese emperors who are hailed as paragons.

Some of the accusations against Jiang Qing were truly ludicrous, and one of my favourites was the occasion when she was said to have insisted that a ring of soldiers should accompany her whilst she was swimming in the sea, in order to act as a shark-barrier! It is undeniable that Jiang Qing was a vengeful and ambitious woman, but if she had not been treated with such scorn by the revolutionary elite during all the years when she was married to Mao, she might not have felt such a burning desire for revenge. She was certainly a mass of contradictions. She believed in the entire population living a life of proletarian purity, whilst her own inclination was for silk sheets and private showings of Greta Garbo films. She decreed proletarian opera for the masses, but had a passion for photographing orchids artistically sprayed with drops of water. One person who met her regularly over a number of years described her to me as rather stupid and very neurotic.

When the Gang of Four was finally put on trial in 1980, it was Jiang Qing's finest hour. There was no doubt that the outcome of the trial had already been decided, as Deng Xiaoping said, before it started, that Mao Zedong would emerge stainless from the trial and that his memory would not be sullied. The defence lawyers, rather than condemning the trial as a travesty of justice, contented themselves with pleading for clemency for those on trial who had shown some contrition. But one has to remember that for years there had not been even a semblance of justice in China. The military and 'the masses' had decided who was guilty and who was innocent, and generally the accused did not even have the benefit of trial by the masses. There was only a handful of lawyers, who had little or no idea of the concept of law. So, given the lack of a legal framework at the time, it was good that there was a trial, even if it was a bad trial.

In promising to preserve Mao's reputation, Deng Xiaoping had reckoned without Jiang Qing. Her defiance at the trial was breathtaking, and not at all what is expected of an accused person in China, where confession of guilt and a plea for clemency are required behaviour. Jiang Qing shouted at the judges, interrupted witnesses, and scandalised everyone. She was unrepentant even in the face of deeply upsetting interrogations of Cultural Revolution victims which she herself had carried out and been unwise enough to record on tape. And then she said what no one wanted to hear. She said that she was merely an assistant to Mao, that she simply fulfilled his orders. Finally she yelled out the memorable sentences 'I was Chairman Mao's dog. Whoever he told me to bite, I bit'. Despite all efforts to prove that Mao had seen through her and warned her back in 1974 'not to form a Gang', no one was convinced. He had kept her in the Politburo together with the other members of the Gang of Four. Eventually Jiang Qing was given the death sentence, suspended for two years dependent on good behaviour. There is no reason to suppose that she has reformed in any way at all, but she was certainly not executed when the two years were up. The other defendants received sentences commensurate with their crimes and degrees of penitence. All of them were very long.

Deng Xiaoping was rehabilitated in the summer of 1977, following a statement in March by Hua Guofeng that all the accusations against Deng were unfounded. At the Third Plenum of the Tenth Central Committee in July that year, Deng was reinstated as Vice-Chairman of the Party. One should not imagine, however, that as soon as the Gang of Four were swept away China immediately returned to normality. The leftist policies were still evident for some time. Hua himself made a rousing speech predicting that 85 per cent of rural land would be mechanised by 1985. To anyone familiar with the lack of mechanisation in China then, and even now, the idea was laughable, and reminiscent of the Great Leap. Even supposing that such a degree of mechanisation were possible in the time, no one seemed to have considered what they would do with the huge labour surplus that would result.

I travelled widely in China in May 1977 with a group of British agricultural experts, and the agricultural policies which were being followed were still very characteristic of the Maoist era. One could hardly expect them to change overnight, but there were some real follies. At an agricultural research institute near Nanjing, which is in the south and usually has a considerable rainfall, we saw the result of Mao's call for each province to be self-sufficient in grain. A great deal of the land had been sown to wheat, which was still quite unripe yet had to be harvested so that the much more important rice crop could be planted in time. When we asked why they grew wheat at all since it was clearly so unsuitable, there was much embarrassed foot-shuffling and quoting of Mao's call to 'Take grain as the key link'.

On that trip we also visited the famous Dazhai Brigade in the poor loess hills of Shanxi. This brigade had always been held up as a model of the collective ideal and the members of the brigade had eschewed any private enterprise whatsoever. Since the accounting was done at brigade level, they had already reached a higher stage than other communes, where accounting was generally done at the lower team level. Dazhai was a byword for gritted teeth and self-sufficiency. But, as we could see, Dazhai was also a victim of its own success. Because the whole country had been told 'In agriculture, learn from Dazhai', they were plagued by thousands of visitors every day, supposedly to learn from their example, but really to enjoy a day out.

The peasants of Dazhai were a tough breed, but it was clear that the vaunted self-sufficiency had been achieved at ridiculous cost. We were told tales of human persistence that were both heroic and foolish. But hard-headed British farmers are not impressed by foolish heroism. They wanted to know why, instead of allowing a wall to be washed away three times by the rain and doggedly rebuilding it each time, the peasants had not immediately telephoned an engineer in the nearest town and asked whether there might not be something wrong with the design of their wall in the first place? Close questioning also revealed that many of the more capital-intensive projects had not been paid for solely from the Dazhai coffers. But I had always admired the hardy leader of the brigade, Chen Yonggui, who at one stage was even made a member of the Politburo, and was sorry to see him eventually labelled too 'leftist' in his views on agriculture. Dazhai, as is the way with the symbols of Chinese politics, was soon to find itself as fiercely pilloried as it was once vaunted.

Everywhere we went that May we heard identical tales of the crimes of the Gang of Four, and especially of Jiang Qing. She had visited Dazhai with a great retinue, and many were the tales we were told of her extravagance and imperiousness. And all over the country we were aware of the cult of Hua Guofeng. His picture hung on walls everywhere, next to

Mao's. Sentences began 'Under the wise leadership of Chairman Hua...'. Hua was now the 'Wise Leader', for only Mao could be the Great Leader.

But however much people sang the praises of Hua Guofeng, one always had the feeling that their hearts were not in it, and they really knew very little about him. Hua himself must have realised that his position was far from secure, and although he remained titular head until 1981 it was actually the politically indestructible Deng Xiaoping who was gathering the reins of government into his hands, and planning a change of direction for China which was awe-inspiring in its daring.

CHAPTER FIVE

REFORM WITHOUT DEMOCRACY

Deng Xiaoping called the the changes which he initiated in 1978 'The Second Revolution', and it had the potential to be a greater revolution than Mao Zedong's in 1949. But the early economic successes, and they were huge, brought with them inflation, price rises and corruption. And, even more importantly, they were not matched by political reforms. There was increasing social discontent, which was dramatically manifested in the mass demonstrations in Peking and many other Chinese cities between April and early June 1989, which were crushed by the Chinese People's Liberation Army. The reasons why Deng Xiaoping's grand plan went so tragically wrong will be discussed in this chapter. Deng's name has appeared throughout this book, and as the past decade has, for better and for worse, belonged to him, now is the time to examine the man and his background.

He was born in the south-west Province of Sichuan in 1904, and although he has always seen himself as a champion of the proletariat, he certainly cannot claim to be a member of it. His father was a landlord, and Deng was the son of his father's second wife (polygamy was still common). Deng Xiaoping began his revolutionary career at the age of sixteen when, like Zhou Enlai, he went to France to study. He worked in the Citroen car factory near Paris, and ran a political newspaper for left-wing Chinese students. He did not devote much time to academic study, but soon became one of the most prominent of the radical Chinese students in Paris.

At the age of twenty-two he spent some months studying in Moscow, at the University of the Toilers of the East, which was set up to train young Asian revolutionaries. After a short spell with the army of the 'Christian Warlord', Feng Yuxiang, Deng travelled down to Guangxi Province in the south of the country, where he became a leading military figure in the Red Army. Indeed at one time Deng was Political Commissar of the whole Red Army. Although his primary task was political training for the troops, he was also an active military man, and led a particularly daring raid on a Japanese airfield during the Anti-Japanese War. When the Communist troops were forced to break out of Yanan in 1947, Deng was one of the two leaders to head the venture. So Deng was no mere military and political theoretician.

It is important to remember that from the 1930s, Deng was an intimate member of Mao Zedong's inner clique, and had distinctly leftist tendencies. Indeed, Mao pointed him out to Nikita Krushchev as a man who would 'go far'. That was before Mao and Deng began to diverge in their policies in the early 1960s. None the less, the man who in the 1980s was to dismantle so much that Mao had erected was once one of his closest 'comrades in arms'.

As pointed out in an earlier chapter, Deng was one of the leading figures in the attacks on the intellectuals in the Anti-Rightist Movement and was a keen supporter of the Great Leap Forward in its initial stages. But it was when Deng Xiaoping saw the devastating results of the ill-conceived movement that he started to move away from his mentor. He realised that the people were starving and that they had to be fed. As an arch-pragmatist, he knew that the policies of the Great Leap had to be discarded, and that material incentives had to be be used to persuade the battered peasants of China to start to produce food again. And his policies worked. Then came the Cultural Revolution in 1966, and as Secretary-General of the Party, Deng was the second most important leader to be disgraced, after Head of State Liu Shaoqi.

Deng was sent to a rugged area of Jiangxi Province in central China where he remained for six years as an ordinary worker. Accompanying him was one of his father's concubines whom he had to look after because she was sick. Then his paralysed son, Deng Pufang, joined them. Deng apparently had to wash him, feed him and generally look after him as well as doing his regular job as a factory worker. Compared with some of his fellow leaders Deng had a relatively easy time. He was not tortured, nor did he die in misery and obscurity. And here one sees the steel of the man, for he was determined to survive. He quite cynically told his children to criticise him publicly in order to save themselves. He wrote a self-criticism, and it is a monument to self-preservation. It is astonishing that any of Deng's critics could have read it without being deeply suspicious. It is so utterly self-abasing, and so full of sickeningly fulsome praise of Mao Zedong that despite the gravity of Deng's situation one cannot help wondering whether he allowed himself a mocking grin as he wrote it. But during the Cultural Revolution the praise of Mao was so extravagant that Deng's would not have seemed out of the ordinary.

Deng returned to power in 1973, and until his next dismissal in April 1976 the Gang of Four mounted a growing clamour of criticism against him. And here we can see what is probably one of Deng's greatest weaknesses – his inability or refusal to recognise a growing movement against him. Or if he did see it, he ignored it, and was caught by surprise in 1976.

Deng's latest disgrace was dealt with in an oddly Chinese way. Instead of being clapped in gaol or held under house arrest, he was allowed to go to the south of the country, where he was looked after by one of the most powerful military leaders in China. And there he waited for the fall of the Gang of Four. Subsequent events showed that not only Deng but many like-minded Chinese leaders were simply waiting for the death of Mao and the removal of the Gang to clear the way for their own return to power. In 1977 Deng was reinstated, and although the colourless Hua Guofeng was titular head of China until his removal in 1981, everyone knew that the true power was Deng Xiaoping.

He is the stuff of which legends are made. He is very small, a man of extraordinary toughness and resilience, and with a surprisingly weak handshake. Much has been said of his chain smoking and his spitting. He enrages Chinese doctors (who are deeply worried about the extent of smoking in China) by claiming that it is his smoking that has helped him to live so long. Having once spent one and a half hours at a meeting with Deng, I can confirm that he always had a cigarette between his fingers, but he only occasionally puffed at it. And although there certainly was a spittoon at his feet, not once did he use it. But his arrogant claim about his smoking is characteristic of the man. He is abrasive and insensitive and, as a result, has made enemies. Mao complained that Deng did not hear what he did not want to hear (he is now very deaf), and that still holds true.

Before the brutal crushing of the pro-democracy demonstrators in Tiananmen Square showed quite a different face to the world, one of the many mistakes made by Western observers when assessing Deng Xiaoping was to assume that he was a liberal. This was a complete misreading of the man. He started the reform programme in China for wholly pragmatic reasons, not because he favoured the more liberal philosophy of the free market. He has little more tolerance of intellectuals than Mao had, but, unlike Mao, he realised that when a socialist society has reached a certain stage of development, then the intellectuals demand more freedom of expression. However, Deng saw this freedom of expression as a tool to further development, and not as an end in itself. He does not view cultural and intellectual freedoms as values in their own right, and he has never hesitated to clamp down on the intellectuals when he considered it necessary. The events of June 1989 were the latest, tragic manifestation of that intolerance.

After the death of Mao Zedong and the removal of the extreme leftists, China was in the grip of an identity crisis. The man who had for so long been the infallible god of his people was dead, the Party was in disarray and the economy clearly needed to be attacked from a fresh angle. Mao's successor, Hua Guofeng, is often described as a 'restorationist', in that he was attached to the main articles of Mao's creed. Later he was to be accused of being a 'whateverist', because he said that whatever Mao said or wrote was right and whatever Mao did was correct and should be followed to the last detail. Hua may not have been as extreme as the Gang of Four, but he leaned towards the Left.

Hua Guofeng must have realised that once Deng Xiaoping was back in the political arena, his own career would be in jeopardy. Although he made trips abroad during his brief years as Party Chairman and Prime Minister, he must have been constantly looking over his shoulder, and with good reason. For Deng Xiaoping and other like-minded individuals were devising an iconoclastic programme of economic and social reform. Much is said about Mr Gorbachev's perestroika, and the word has now entered the English language. No one, except the Chinese, has ever heard of *gaige*, the Chinese equivalent, and yet Deng Xiaoping's reforms predate those of Gorbachev by some seven years. The Russians have borrowed from the Chinese experience of reform, and have watched the developments in China with burning interest. The success or failure of the Chinese experiment has vital implications for the Soviet Union and its reformers.

In the late 1970s Deng Xiaoping launched what were called the Four Modernisations. These were the modernisation of agriculture, industry, science and technology and national defence. These had already been mooted in the 1960s, and Zhou Enlai raised them again in 1975 as the rubric under which 'productive forces' were to be developed. The Four Modernisations were to transform all aspects of the Chinese economy, and were to propel China into the twenty-first century as the embryo of an industrial giant.

In some ways the Chinese reformers in the late 1970s were faced with the same problem as Mao Zedong in the late 1950s – how to stimulate agricultural and industrial output. But where Mao relied on mass mobilisation, Deng and his disciples went for a less idealistic option. They accepted that man cannot live by ideology alone, and that if he is offered incentives, then he may be prepared to produce more. The reforms which were launched at the watershed Third Plenum of the Eleventh Central Committee in December 1978 were predicated on three main proposals: material incentives should be used as the principal stimulus to induce greater productivity and efficiency; market forces should be allowed to influence the price and availability of goods; private ownership could play a useful role in a socialist economy. The aim of the reforms was to improve people's livelihood as well as the country's economic performance, and in this they achieved notable successes.

All of the proposals for reform conflicted with long-held tenets of socialism, and have indeed been the subject of an extremely lively debate that has raged in China over the past ten years, and will probably continue to rage with even greater intensity. The reforms started in the rural sector, which comprises some 80 per cent of the country's population. In the initial stages of the reforms, first production teams (the smallest unit in a commune) and then individual families were allotted a production quota (for grain, for example) and then were allowed to keep anything they could produce over and above the quota. Previously, everything produced by a production team or brigade was handed over to the commune, which then gave back a certain amount of grain according to the number of work points which a person had earned during the year. It is often said now that that system was ultra-egalitarian, as everyone earned the same. This is not strictly true, as a person could earn from seven to fourteen work points per day. However, it is true in the sense that no one was going to get rich even if he or she worked considerably harder than any other member of the team. There was certainly a lot of shirking, and peasants resented the fact that they were no longer allowed the traditional Chinese winter slack season. Instead they were expected to use that time for repair and renewal of irrigation systems, dams, and anything else necessary for agricultural production. And vital work it was.

The reform of the agricultural system at the end of the 1970s took off with a bang. Understandably, there was a great deal of initial suspicion on the part of the peasants. There had been so many changes of policy over the decades, and from one year to the next they had carried out Party instructions that were subsequently rescinded. But gradually a few of the bolder spirits took the government at its word, and started to increase their output sharply. Having fulfilled the quota they then sold their surplus produce either in the burgeoning rural markets, or by the roadside. I saw the first signs of this extraordinary change in March 1979 when I was in the south-western Province of Sichuan. Lining the rural roadsides were huge numbers of peasants selling poultry, eggs and vegetables, medicinal herbs, rat poison (its efficacy demonstrated by artistically arrayed rat corpses) and a miscellany of other produce. The roads through the small towns were jammed on market day, and one was immediately aware that something truly revolutionary was happening. I did wonder whether there was really a market for so many similar goods, and the still-full baskets of some of the peasants at the end of the day seemed to justify that doubt.

As the peasants gained confidence, agricultural production started to soar and the reforms moved several steps forward. In 1983 the government announced that the 'household responsibility system' as it was called, would be universally applied. Peasants had by that stage been allocated land to till on a rental basis. Initially everyone was given a piece of good land, a piece of medium and a piece of poor. Naturally this caused problems, as sometimes the pieces of land were some distance apart, and people started to exchange with each other. A further complication was that the peasants were unhappy about having to rotate the land every few years, which had been the initial plan. After all, why waste money and effort bringing a piece of land to a state of maximum fertility, only to hand it over to someone else? So some of them exhausted the land by applying too much fertiliser, and some leased the land to a neighbour and went off to do something more lucrative. In 1984 the government announced that the division of land as it stood then would hold good for fifteen years. And indeed in many areas it is now allocated virtually in perpetuity. (However, some areas still abide by the three-year rotation system, as they consider it to be fairer.) That same year saw a record grain crop of 407 million tons, a great increase over the 304 million tons produced in 1978.

All these changes sounded the death knell of the commune system. The communes have been disbanded, and their adminstrative functions transferred to townships or village committees. The system which sympathetic left-wing foreigners regarded as the essence of all that was good in socialism has been eradicated with an ease that seems incredible when one remembers the turmoil that accompanied its birth. Of all the changes that have happened in the past decade, the end of the commune system would be seen by Maoists as the definitive sign that one era of Chinese socialism has come to an end and another begun.

The agricultural reforms worked well in the initial stages because the foundation was already there. Chinese peasants have been farming for thousands of years, and have a great understanding of their land. Now the government was simply asking them to do something at which they were already expert. Anyone who has travelled through rural China has seen the peasants working relentlessly in daunting climatic conditions. The knowledge that the traditionally hard work was now going to lead to greater wealth was a very attractive proposition.

In 1985, emboldened by the sharp increase in agricultural output, the government replaced the compulsory grain purchase quotas with a more flexible procurement system, and announced that it would sign contracts with the peasants for grain, cotton and similar products. The peasants were free to sign, or not to sign. The system immediately ran into trouble. The grain harvest fell by 6 per cent as peasants turned to more profitable cash crops. Peasants soon found, especially if they lived near a city, that the big money was to be found in fish farming, fruit growing (free-market fruit is always much better than the bruised products to be found in the state shops), vegetable growing and cut or potted flowers.

The government was faced with a painful dilemma. If it backtracked on the reforms, the peasants' faith and enthusiasm would be severely dented. If it let the price of grain float up to a more realistic level to encourage production, then there would be discontent amongst the city dwellers. It was the classic problem that faces every socialist country when trying to reform a system which has been based for years on high state subsidies and low consumer prices. As the countries of the Eastern bloc learnt to their cost, a rise in food prices leads to disturbing social rumblings. China has now learnt the same lesson.

Immediately the drop in grain production became apparent, the Chinese government changed the ratio of its purchasing prices so that grain farmers would not lose out, and increased the availability of agricultural inputs, such as fertiliser. But this did not bring about the wished-for upturn in grain production, and China has still not managed to produce a harvest equal to that of 1984. No matter what the government does to persuade the Chinese to grow grain, very few will be willing to engage in tough, unremunerative labour when there are easier ways to make money.

From the early 1980s the signs of increased wealth in the countryside were highly visible. The first purchase was generally a television set, even if reception was poor. New bicycles abounded. Small tractors were a most desirable item, although used mainly for haulage. But it was the new housing that was the real sign of wealth. Depending on the region of China, it could be a large, simple, handsome wooden structure, or something more opulent in brick and stone. In 1984 the diminutive Party chief, Hu Yaobang, had said that the aim of the reforms was 'to make people rich'. People were urged to emulate the so-called 'ten thousand yuan households': households which were earning at least that in a year. When one bears in mind that the official poverty line in China is a per capita income of less than 200 yuan per annum one can appreciate that 10 000 yuan bestows a quite luxurious standard of living. (At present £1 = 6.3 yuan). It is now common to see a dazzling array of consumer goods in peasant households, ranging from videos and hi-fi sets to elaborate furniture and powerful Japanese motorbikes.

A number of households soon attained this degree of wealth, and now one of the major contradictions in the new system began to show itself. Shortly after the reforms were launched, the drive to restrict families to just one child gained momentum. Under any circumstances this would have appeared draconian in a society which is not only traditionally fond of children and where people, especially in the rural areas, tend to produce several, but it also clashed with the new material aspirations of the peasants. The simple fact is, the more manpower there is in a family, the greater its potential to generate wealth. From everything that I have seen in Chinese villages, it is clear that the families who were lucky enough to have produced several children before the birth-control policy was implemented are growing rich quickly, whilst the families with only one child, and a girl into the bargain, are severely disadvantaged. Traditionally, when a girl marries, she marries out of her own family and into her husband's, so her own parents have lost her labour-power. This partly accounts for the traditional Chinese peasant preference for boy children. Furthermore, in a country which as yet has very little in the way of social security, peasants need to be looked after by their children in their old age, and a girl who has 'married out' may not be able to do this.

The larger families soon contracted to become 'specialised households', supplying only one kind of goods to the state, ranging from tobacco to imitation Tang Dynasty horses, and becoming very wealthy in the process. But the real lords of wealth are those who have a vehicle, for not only do they transport their own family's produce, but everyone else's too. If there is a scarcity of any particular goods the truck drivers have the power to remedy the hiatus. But again, a family needs money to buy a truck, and the labour-power to generate that money.

One must have some sympathy with the present Chinese government and its attempt to limit the Chinese population, for they inherited another of Mao Zedong's mistakes. Mao had always declared that there could not be too many Chinese, and any attempt to control the population was a Malthusian nonsense. Now the Chinese have a population of over 1100 million people. Earlier prognostications that the population would be 1.2 billion by the turn of the century have already been discarded, and it is admitted that it will be at least 1.3 billion. The population is growing by 20 million per annum, and a growth rate of that order requires nearly 7 million tons of grain each year to feed it. With 20 per cent of the world's population to feed from less than 5 per cent of the world's arable land, small wonder that the government is anxious.

Although the birth-control policy has been largely successful in the cities, where tiny flats and financial penalties are a great inducement to people to limit their families, the government admits that it has failed in the countryside. It is now acknowledged that local officials have lied about statistics, and that far more children are being born than was earlier realised. Now the government has relaxed the policy, and accepts that under certain conditions families may have a second child. For example, if both parents are only children, and their first child is a girl, then they may try for a second. But no one is supposed to have a third child. This is simply bowing to the inevitable, but it is also over-optimistic, as large numbers of rural families have produced three or more children despite the ban. If a rich family is fined for producing a second or third child, it gladly pays up, and the poor families feel that they are already so poor they have little to lose. Although the population growth is a major problem for China, at least the present relaxation should mean fewer cases of female infanticide and abortion of female foetuses.

Once the reforms in agriculture were well under way, it was

the turn of the industrial sector. The industrial reforms had already started some years earlier in selected areas such as Sichuan. That province had been run by Deng Xiaoping's protégé Zhao Ziyang, until the latter took over from Hua Guofeng as Prime Minister in 1980. The essence of the industrial reforms, promulgated in October 1984, was the gradual emergence of industrial enterprises from the stranglehold of the Party and the state. That was not to say that state enterprises would suddenly become privatised (although some of the more radical reformers have proposed just such a move), but that enterprise managers would have a much greater say in running their factories. Where the state had previously taken the entire profit of the enterprise and then handed back a portion for wages, welfare, capital investment and so forth, the factory would now be able to keep a much larger percentage of its profit after paying a specified amount of tax to the state. Where the factory's Communist Party Committee used to meddle in management, now a new breed of commercially minded managers was to be fostered. There was to be much less central control, market mechanisms were to apply to a certain extent and, in theory, factory managers were to be responsible for the hiring and firing of staff. Where previously enterprise employees had life tenure and their children often took over their jobs when they retired, from 1985 a contract system was introduced for new staff. However, a recent visit to the huge State Capital Iron and Steel Works in Peking revealed that jobs were still being handed down from parent to child.

Where any form of private enterprise had been regarded as anti-socialist and capitalist during the Cultural Revolution, it was now encouraged. This was especially true of the service industries, which were seen as a home for some of China's enormous surplus labour. Each year millions of young people were leaving school with no job prospects. They were euphemistically called 'waiting-for-employment youth'.

All this was to change after 1984, and certain benefits were immediately apparent. In China's cities there had never been enough services. In cheap restaurants people used to stand behind each other's chairs, waiting for their turn to sit down. There were queues for a hair cut. It took weeks to get a garment made or a pair of shoes repaired. There was only a tiny number of snack stalls of the kind that abound in Taiwan, Hong Kong or anywhere else where there is a large Chinese community. Before the reforms it had always seemed to me that the purpose of Chinese socialism had been to make life as inconvenient as possible for those who lived under it.

Understandably, the urban Chinese, like their rural counterparts, were initially suspicious of the reforms and the uncertainty which they brought with them. For decades they had been used to the so-called 'iron rice-bowl', which meant that no one was ever sacked, no matter how idle; no factory ever closed, no matter how inefficient. Suddenly life was full of possibilities and uncertainties, including the freedom to choose one's job, and the freedom to be thrown out of it. Many rose to the challenge, and the Chinese entrepreneurial spirit came to the fore. There were many tales of successful groups of young entrepreneurs. One such group had borrowed a small sum from the bank and set up a tea stall which soon mushroomed into a supermarket. The Chinese press praised them for having actually found out what their customers wanted to buy, rather than stacking the shelves with goods which then gathered dust.

Millionaires sprang up overnight. There was the man who remembered a famous recipe for chicken, and opened a restaurant to serve the dish. He bought up every chicken in the district and boarded them all over his house, including his grandmother's room. He was hoping to capitalise on a similarly famous pork dish, but did not think that his family would take so kindly to pigs in every room. A woman on the outskirts of Peking became a wealthy egg producer (eggs had previously been rationed), and gained fame and envy by being one of the first Chinese to own a private car (Japanese, of course). Another man produced a sharp line in shirts, and the moment that particular model became really popular and everyone was clamouring for it, immediately changed to another style. All these potential industrial magnates were held up for emulation in much the same way as the model soldier, worker or peasant had been in Mao's day. These were the new model socialists.

Life has not been easy for the new entrepreneurs. One of them told me that his attempt to start up and expand an audio-visual business was fraught with difficulties. When he started up on his own there were still no laws governing private enterprise, and he faced enormous problems when dealing with local bureaucrats. They quite arbitrarily taxed him for 85-90 per cent of his profit, and he had no means of redress.

Deng Xiaoping himself said that socialism cannot be considered superior to capitalism if it keeps people poor. He acknowledged that under the reforms some people and some regions would get rich before others, but the only alternative was to keep everyone poor. And anyway the benefits would gradually seep through to the disadvantaged – the well-known policy of 'trickle-down'.

Even more radical ideas followed, one of which was the proposal that China should pass a bankruptcy law. There has always been enormous inefficiency in many of China's state enterprises, but the idea that the state could declare its own factories bankrupt and its employees redundant was quite shocking to those who believe that a guaranteed job is one of the most fundamental rights of a citizen in a socialist state. As with so many of the reforms, the experiment was started in one particular area only, in this case in the north-eastern industrial city of Shenyang. Factories which had been doing consistently badly were given a 'yellow card', which warned them that unless they improved their financial situation they would be closed and their staff laid off. Any workers who lost their jobs were to be paid around 70 per cent of their previous wages for a certain period of time, but not indefinitely. Some factories took on new managers and turned their factories round. But some actually did close, and about 63 000 people in Shenyang lost their jobs. Ironically, many factories were anxious to be issued with the 'yellow card' because it meant that during the probationary period they were given tax holidays and low-interest loans.

There was considerable resistance to the bankruptcy law, and the National People's Congress, China's parliament, threw it out several times before it was finally passed in 1988 in a 'trial' form. Now it remains to be seen how vigorously it will be enacted. It could be argued that in a country which still has an irrational pricing and distribution system it is unfair to blame enterprises for the chaos which often ensues. Frequently the management of a factory is passed from one government department to another, and the factory managers never know which is really in charge. Furthermore, and this is the crucial difference between the agricultural and the industrial reforms, China always had a solid agricultural base, which the industrial sector did not. After the Communists took over they adopted the highly centralised, planned Soviet system, with its emphasis on heavy industry and capital investment. Factory managers were not expected to show any initiative; quite the reverse. And suddenly, from 1984, they were being asked to show all the flair of capitalist entrepreneurs.

Here however, is where many Western commentators have made a fundamental mistake in assessing the reforms in China. There is nothing that the denizens of a particular political system like more than the belief that those who live under a different system are at last beginnning to see the light, and are becoming more 'like us'. Many newspaper headlines proclaimed that China was becoming capitalist. This was by no means the case. The private sector still only accounts for about 5 per cent of urban employment and industrial production. Detailed annual plans are drawn up and the country still operates on a Five-Year Plan. However, China has moved towards a much more mixed economy, which combines state planning and central regulation with an increasing reliance on market forces and a fusion of state, collective and private ownership. What the leadership wanted to see was a more-ruthlessly efficient approach to enterprise management, and one that reflected the capitalist managerial approach with profit as its buzzword. But the Chinese leadership also argued that as long as the means of ownership were still largely in the hands of the state and the collective, China was still socialist.

The immediate result of allowing enterprises to keep a substantial part of their profits was a sharp drop in state revenues, and a parallel jump in the wages bill. By 1985 the latter had leapt up 17 per cent because enterprises were now permitted to pay bonuses. Decentralisation of industrial planning led to a runaway increase in industrial production in 1984 and 1985. The gross value of industrial output showed an increase of 18 per cent in 1985, well over twice what the government had planned. Because of China's weak infrastructure this meant that unwanted goods piled up at the factories, there was an acute shortage of raw materials, and unchecked provincial spending of foreign currency led to a sharp increase in the trade deficit and a drain on the foreign exchange reserves. The foreign trade deficit in 1985 was US $11.2 billion, which is small compared with that of many countries, but did mean that China had to start borrowing abroad. This was extremely worrying for a country which since 1949 had prided itself on not being in the thrall of foreign bankers.

The government was forced to introduce a greater measure of central control. There was much tighter central management of foreign exchange reserves, and a curb on imports. Since a large proportion of China's imports were from Japan, that was the country hardest hit by the clamp-down, and 1985 saw a series of demonstrations, mainly by Chinese students, condemning Japan's 'economic imperialism'. But here lies one of the many problems which have resulted from the reforms. Too much money was chasing too few much-coveted foreign consumer goods. There was spiralling inflation and sharp price rises.

The past decade in China has been characterised by the leadership's attempts to forge ahead with plans to mould China into a developed industrial country, whilst at the same time trying to pre-empt or ameliorate the problems that have inevitably arisen. But was the leadership united in its aims? I think it is fair to say that even now the top leadership is committed to economic reform. Where they have differed, and will continue to differ is on the pace and extent of reform. At the Thirteenth Party Congress in October 1987, Deng Xiaoping retired from the Politburo in order to force the more cautious reformers in his own age bracket to do the same. These more cautious people included the veteran economic planner Chen Yun, the former Mayor of Peking Peng Zhen, who had returned to power after the Cultural Revolution, in addition to hardline ideologues. But Peng Zhen, Chen Yun and other conservatives returned to political eminence during the infighting which resulted from the crisis engendered by the pro-democracy demonstrations.

By the late 1980s the reforms had run into serious trouble, with soaring inflation, runaway capital investment, severe energy shortages and rampant corruption. Whilst Mao Zedong was alive China had been poor, austere and cowed, yet remained a byword for honesty and integrity. Lost property was returned, theft was uncommon. Such a state of affairs may partly have been due to the repressive policies of the time, but there is no doubt that many believed that in a socialist society people did not steal from or cheat each other. But the economic reforms in China gave rise to an obsessive desire for wealth and for material possessions. Mammon ruled. It is only natural that as people acquire greater prosperity they are also going to want the outward manifestations of that wealth, such as television sets, washing machines, even cars. They want better housing and better opportunities. The government would not deny them such aspirations. But matters went much further than that. Corruption on a massive scale invaded every area of life and society. Crime escalated, and a dog-eat-dog attitude began to prevail.

The exhortation to 'get rich' in 1984 and the calls to emulate the 'ten thousand yuan' families were soon seen to have been conveying the wrong messages. The government began to call on everyone to remember spiritual values, socialist ethics and good-neighbourly virtues. But these admonitions fell on stony ground. Initially the corruption was small-scale. A professor grumbled to me that he could not even get a book out of the library without administering a small bribe to the librarian. Irritating perhaps, but not the stuff of which social collapse is made. Soon the scale of bribery and corruption reached staggering proportions, and China was at a stage when nothing could be achieved without a bribe. The best goods were kept hidden in a back room until some extra payment was made. Rail tickets were not available without a back-hander. Jobs were saved for the children of those who could offer something in return. And although everyone professed to be appalled by what was happening, they all admitted to being co-conspirators, because if they stood on the high moral ground they lost out all round.

There are many reasons why this has happened. China is a society where goods and services are still in very short supply, although the situation is much better than it was a decade ago. Officials are badly paid, but they have power. If a would-be entrepreneur wants to start a small factory, he needs planning permission and a licence. So he goes to the relevant local office to get one. The man in charge has the power to grant or deny the licence, but his salary is low and he cannot afford the colour television that his family badly wants. So all sorts of difficulties arise over granting the licence until the applicant understands what is required and makes a suitable offering. Then the licence is granted. Or the factory manager of a state enterprise is desperate for some raw materials in short supply, and knows that another factory has them. He approaches the factory and finds that the manager does not necessarily want money, but his son wants a job in the factory run by the supplicant. The deal is done. These may be minor examples, but they are typical.

There have been a large number of cases of bribery and corruption on a breathtaking scale, and many of these have resulted from China's two-tiered pricing system. Under the state pricing system, state-run enterprises are given raw materials at a subsidised price and sell their state production quota at a fixed, subsidised price. Non-state sectors of industry have to pay a higher price. Any production by the state sector over and above its quota, can also be sold at the market price. So the inevitable result is that those who have access to goods at state-subsidised prices sell them on the open market at the higher price, and make a substantial profit, whilst actually cheating the state. Meanwhile, state enterprises are deprived of raw materials. As an example, in the spring of 1989, state enterprises in cities like Shanghai and Peking were acutely short of coal because it had been bought for a higher price by local authorities whilst in transit from the coal fields.

One of the most spectacular cases of corruption occurred in 1985 on the island of Hainan, which lies off the south China coast. This is a very backward area, with a weak infrastructure. It was recently declared a province, and the government hopes to turn it into a Special Economic Zone like the ones near Hong Kong, in order to attract foreign capital. The leaders of Hainan were told to develop the island as quickly as possible, but no one told them how to do it. Showing considerable acumen they imported large quantities of Japanese cars and television sets and then exported them on to the mainland, selling them for a colossal profit. Although to us this would seem like normal business practice, it was against the Chinese regulations and action was immediately taken against the ringleaders. However, the government now seems to have acknowledged that, as they did not do it for private profit, their crime was not so great, and several have been reinstated.

Much worse cases came to light. In north-east China for example, a woman official and her accomplices accumulated hundreds of thousands of yuan through corrupt practices, and were executed for it. Day after day one read in the Chinese press cases of people who swelled their bank accounts with money from bribes or embezzlement. Some of the sums involved were small, but some were spectacularly large, running into hundreds of thousands, or even millions of yuan. There are now much stiffer penalties for crimes of corruption, and the law lays down very specific degrees of punishment for the amount embezzled. If someone has benefited to the tune of 10 000 yuan or more, he may be sentenced to death or life imprisonment. However, it is now stated that everyone is equal before the law, but this is far from being the case. Many high-ranking officials involved in large-scale corruption cases were merely dismissed from their posts, or given light prison sentences, whilst less important people were sentenced to life imprisonment or death. This disparity of treatment caused great discontent and increasing cynicism amongst the general population.

Society rapidly divided into the haves and have-nots, and this is where so much of the tension arose. The Chinese call jealousy the 'red-eyed disease' and it is endemic. At first the city dwellers were consumed with jealousy of the new-found wealth of the peasants, who had already benefited from the reforms. Then as the reforms started in the industrial sector, the white-collar workers became envious of the increased wages and bonuses of the factory workers. In recent years many teachers have grumbled to me that apart from extra teaching or translation work they have no prospects of increasing their income. The new rich now are undoubtedly the small traders in the cities where there are market stalls selling everything from clothes to food. These stalls are owned by hard-eyed young men with fashionable clothes and hair-styles, who would sell their own grandmothers for a profit.

When the stallholders first appeared everyone was delighted. They offered better goods in greater variety than the state shops. This soon turned sour. The red-eyed disease has blinded people to the benefits. Now all they do is quote the scandal stories: the dumpling stallholder who poisoned a hundred people by using meat which the meat inspectors had already condemned in a state market, the clothes that fell apart after two washings, the shoes which wore through in a week, the gadget that promised to make a person grow five centimetres a year, but in reality burnt the skin and brought the gullible purchaser out in spots; the fruit that was excellent, but so expensive that only a fellow entrepreneur could afford it. They grumble that the stallholders buy in bulk, store the goods until a shortage has forced the prices up, and then put them on the market at five times the pre-shortage price. All the stories are perfectly true, and the government has tried hard to crack down on these speculators who are forcing up the cost-of-living index. But the real problem is that the government has to decide whether it has the courage to rely wholly on market forces or not. Even before the mass demonstrations in April and May 1989 it had not done so.

But the government found that having opened the Pandora's box of economic reform, it was not going to be easy to close it again. Many of the provinces have now become 'independent kingdoms'. They cling on to their own revenues. In 1988 a general audit revealed provincial and enterprise tax evasion amounting to billions of yuan. Where previously most of the silk in China was taken to factories in Shanghai and Hangzhou to be processed, now the provinces would not let it pass the provincial boundaries. They wanted to reap the financial benefits of processing it and exporting it themselves, even if their factories were not as skilled as those in Shanghai. There were even road-blocks to prevent raw materials leaving counties and provinces.

At the lower level, the counties gained considerable power over their own development, and even villages were becoming largely autonomous. Village-level industry has shown a tremendous expansion over the past decade, and has pushed total rural output up by 10.5 per cent per annum. Some villages now have almost no agricultural output, or are paying just one or two families to produce grain. And some villages have grown very rich indeed, with three-storey houses, some even with garages and the cars to put in them. In 1988 for the first time, industrial output outstripped agricultural output in the countryside.

With the disbandment of the communes and the transfer of their functions to the townships, many of the former commune leaders, frequently very able people, came to see their job as fixer for the village enterprises. Because of their past responsibilities they had excellent connections amongst the officials running the local planning departments and the banks. The central government might decide that there was too much capital investment (it rose at an alarming and uncontrollable rate) and forbid the banks to lend money for capital projects. But the local leader is an old friend of the bank manager, and persuades or coerces him into giving the loan. The village secures the loan, so that even if the project fails, the bank does not lose out. New projects also enjoy low-interest loans and tax holidays.

Meanwhile, all the uncontrolled development was leading to acute shortages of raw materials, uneven development, unwanted surpluses and a bad pollution problem. The disparity between the rich coastal areas and the poor inland areas was growing more acute year by year. The leadership argued that there would inevitably be 'trickle-down', and that the poor provinces would eventually benefit. But this requires a much more efficient taxation system. At present very few private individuals pay tax, and the problem of setting up a national tax-collecting system is a daunting one. Even the simplest system would be difficult to implement in a country where at least one fifth of the population is illiterate. And the provincial and county governments would not show excessive zeal in collecting taxes intended for central government. The contrast between the coastal and inland areas is acute, and the contrast is even sharper in the Special Economic Zones which have been established in China's coastal areas. These areas were set up to attract foreign investment and joint ventures. Wages and salaries are much higher than in other parts of China, and many people regard them as the blueprint for China's future economic development.

In the coastal areas people are well-dressed, well-fed and, in the adjacent rural areas, increasingly well-housed. In the western and north-western areas, and in many of the central provinces there is still extreme poverty and many people live a primitive existence. Many have no cash income at all, and rely wholly on government subsidies. At least 30 million have problems feeding and clothing themselves. In 1988 the government warned that after a year of disastrous drought and flooding, some 20 million faced starvation, and many more faced food shortages. China may not swarm with beggars as do so many developing countries, but they certainly exist and their numbers are increasing rapidly. The large cities have increasingly big floating populations, sometimes as high as 10 per cent of the total. These people do not have residence permits, so they do not have rations cards for the city. This means that they have to live by their wits and by doing temporary jobs, usually on construction sites. They are frequently exploited and paid little for a very long day's work, and have no social security. Earlier in 1989, in an attempt to curb excessive capital investment, the government cancelled hundreds of state construction projects and sent the itinerant labourers back to their villages. One could hardly walk through Peking railway station for the thousands of workers sleeping on their bedrolls.

The Chinese government was walking a perilous tightrope. It did not want to reimpose control, but feared that social chaos might ensue if it were to let market forces rule completely. In 1988, when it was clear that inflation was going to be at least 20 per cent for the whole year, (that was the official figure, in reality it was certainly much nearer 30 per cent) the government reluctantly reimposed price controls over seventy-two major commodities. These included grain, fertiliser, oil grains, steel and a wide range of other essential goods and foodstuffs. The government was extremely worried that if food prices continued to rise, then there would be the same kind of social disorder seen in the past in some Eastern bloc countries. Indeed it was so worried that the man in charge of law and security matters, Politburo member Qiao Shi, was sent to several Eastern Bloc countries including Poland, to study their methods of riot control. A group of Chinese military were also sent to Poland, the United States, and some West European countries to examine riot control methods and to purchase the relevant equipment.

It is perhaps ludicrous to hark back to a time of revolutionary purity under Mao Zedong. But then society was characterised by plain living, and for many people a genuine belief in the slogan 'Serve the People', which was printed on anything from cooking pots to tea mugs. China may have been pure, but it was drab. The reforms brought colour and choice, at a price. Gangs hung around on street corners and young men murmured 'Change money, change money' to any foreigner who passed. When you bought something from a private trader you could haggle over it. You could buy a duck-down anorak or some silk underwear from a market stall for a fraction of the price charged by the state stores. The labels proclaimed the Western clothes designer for which they were manufactured. If you wanted something made it could be done in days instead of weeks. There was a much more 'can do' attitude about the country, almost reminiscent of Hong Kong. This however, applied largely to the private and collective sectors, rather than the state sector.

When I lived in Peking in the early 1970s it was almost impossible to get anything to eat after about 7 p.m. except at the mule-drivers' cafes. These stayed open all night, and did a good line in draught beer and dumplings. The reforms brought new joint-venture or private restaurants which remained open until midnight. There were tables full of well-dressed young men and women, eating dishes that, by Chinese standards, were very expensive indeed. Yet they had rolls of money in their pockets, smoked sought-after brands of Western cigarettes, and had a swagger about them that was quite new.

This caused much social tension. No matter how well a white-collar worker does his or her job, he or she will never be able to afford that kind of meal in that kind of restaurant. But the white-collar worker does have other things to offer, as discussed earlier. China has always been a country which has run on *guanxi* or 'connections', and never more so than during the past decade with the easing of moral and social constraints. Now though, the burden on those who have something to give, whether it is a flat, a job, a trip abroad, is overwhelming. Chinese have told me that no approach, however innocent it may seem, can be taken at face value. Everybody needs favours, and any favour that one asks for oneself will be called in at some future date, no matter how distant.

Foreigners in China gradually became more wary. Some years before one might have felt that Chinese befriended one out of intellectual or social curiosity, or simply because they liked one, but now one realised that the reasons might be rather different. Soon after an introduction was made the requests would start. Could one arrange for a scholarship for themselves, their children, their nephews or nieces? Could one bring in a cassette recorder for them on one's next trip? Could one exchange some 'foreign exchange certificates' for ordinary yuan? (The government introduced a two-tier system of currency, of nominally the same face value, to obviate a black market in currency. It has had exactly the opposite effect.) I have to stress that this did not always happen, but it happened with increasing regularity and it made one feel very uncomfortable to have to say no. Overseas Chinese lamented the fact that when they went to China to visit relatives they were sent a shopping list of expensive electronic goods which the family wanted, often to the tune of several thousand US dollars. A number of overseas Chinese told me that they had no intention of returning to China as long as this grasping attitude continued.

Even Chinese students studying abroad on very small stipends were living below the poverty line because their relatives expected them to take home either a large sum in foreign currency, or consumer goods of the same value. To do this, four graduate students might live in one room, eat a poor diet, and not spend any money at all on travel or learning about the culture of the country in which they were studying.

Even before the mass demonstrations showed the extent of popular dissatisfaction, the Chinese government was extremely worried about the negative image of corruption. Both the moderate and radical wings of the leadership recognised it as one of the major problems of the present time. The Chinese leadership still maintained that China was a socialist country, and that its socialist image was being severely damaged by such corrupt practices. Characteristically, they blamed 'Western bourgeois decadent influences' for the current state of affairs. But the West was simply being used as a scapegoat. The leadership knew perfectly well that the Chinese are capable of being corrupt without any help, and the existing practices were no different from those prevalent before 1949.

Both the leadership and the general population watched the soaring crime rate with alarm. In 1988 the overall crime rate was up by 45 per cent on 1987, with the majority being economic crimes. Serious crime rose by 65 per cent. Crimes committed by Party members were a particular worry for the leadership. In 1983 the Party launched a 'rectification campaign' against its 48 million members. Every Party member (at least half of whom had joined the Party during the Cultural Revolution) was investigated. The rectification lasted for nearly four years, and was moderate and gradual. Of 325 000 members who received some form of disciplinary action, only 200 000 were dismissed — a very small number given the Party's size.

Prostitution, eradicated after 1949, returned with miniskirted girls offering themselves for sums ranging from 50 to 1000 yuan per night. Many had pimps. Venereal disease was on the increase. Violent crime rose sharply, and highway robbery and mugging on trains became increasingly common. Even drug dealing was on the increase, albeit on a tiny scale. The government reacted firmly to this criminal upsurge, and every week one heard of anything from seven to seventeen criminals being executed in one of the major cities. There were executions for crimes ranging from murder to rape to the somewhat indeterminate charge of 'hooliganism'. Execution is by a bullet in the back of the head.

Even before June 1989, the number of judicial executions in China was causing great anxiety amongst international human rights organisations. Whenever someone is executed in the United States there is immense international publicity, but hardly a line was written about similar events in China. A well-placed source estimates that as many as 10 000 people may have been executed in China in 1988.

And yet to give credit where credit's due, the attitude towards the rule of law changed significantly during the 1980s. It was acknowledged that the terrible excesses of the Cultural Revolution happened because men, rather than laws, governed the way the country was run. Over the past ten years China has enacted a whole series of new laws. Where there were only 2000 lawyers in 1980, now there are at least 25 000. There is still not a clear enough line between the party and the judiciary, but at present China is experimenting with the principle of an independent judiciary, although it remains to be seen how far that idea will now progress. Judges are frequently not party members, and lawyers have learnt that it is their duty actively to defend their clients, and not merely to plead for clemency. The job of a lawyer is not an easy one. An accused person is considered guilty until proved innocent, and of the total number brought to trial only a tiny proportion are found not guilty. There have been many instances of official interference in the judicial procedure, and in the spring of 1989 a Professor of Law told me that in some cases the verdict was decided even before the trial took place. The Chinese leaders were, however, acutely conscious of the need to establish a legal system which would be credible not only in the eyes of their own people, but also in the eyes of the foreigners who wanted to do business with them. Stories abounded of contracts arbitrarily broken by the Chinese companies, and even foreign businessmen who had been trading with China for decades were alarmed and angered by this situation.

The economic reforms proceeded apace, and brought with them both real successes and real problems. But the spectre which rose to haunt China's leaders even before the reforms were properly launched was a popular demand for greater democracy. A decade later this was to lead to great tragedy. The pro-democracy demonstrations in Tiananmen Square between April and early June 1989 were the most dramatic manifestation of public discontent with the way China was being ruled. However, they were the culmination of a series of lesser waves of unrest. The first powerful challenge to the post-Mao leadership's monolithic power came in 1978 with the birth of 'Democracy Wall' as it was called. This was a wall in Peking where mainly young people stuck up posters airing their views and demanding greater freedom of expression. Those who first used the wall to state their demands for political and social change, and the editors of the dissident magazines which sprang up at the same time, were generally workers rather than intellectuals. But in China many young people started to work in factories during the Cultural Revolution when such work was considered glorious, and yet their parents were often high-ranking members. So the offspring came from highly-politicised backgrounds, and often had access to Party publications not available to the rest

Deng Xiaoping presiding over the opening of the 13th Congress of the Chinese Communist Party in 1987

(Top) A newly rich peasant's house in south-west China
(Bottom left) Blocks of workers' flats built recently in the north-east city of Harbin
(Bottom right) The lobby of the Great Wall Hotel in Peking

(Top and bottom) Modern and traditional methods of ploughing exist side by side

(Top) The well-stocked supermarket is a symbol of the economic reforms
(Bottom) The economic reforms have encouraged private entrepreneurs

(Top) Couples are exhorted to produce only one child
(Bottom left) The single-child policy is producing a generation of 'little Emperors and Empresses'
(Bottom right) Newly-weds hire Western clothes for a wedding photograph

Students take over Tiananmen Square in May 1989

(Top) A man confronts Chinese tanks in the aftermath of the Tiananmen Square massacre in June 1989
(Bottom) Students crushed by army tanks in Tiananmen Square

Students erect a 30-foot-high polystyrene 'Goddess of Democracy' modelled on the Statue of Liberty

of the population. These young dissidents had not studied abroad, but had received their political training during the Cultural Revolution. They had learned the freedom to speak out and had travelled the country and seen that despite two and a half decades of socialism, there were still areas of grinding poverty. Furthermore, as mentioned in Chapter 4, the Tiananmen Incident in April 1976 had already provided a boost to the independent thinking of the young. Although the main spokesmen of the 1978 democracy movement often had differing philosophical orientations, they stressed various common themes. These included and indeed centred around democracy, civil liberties, the right to employment and the importance of the state meeting the basic economic needs of the people.

The most famous of the Democracy Wall dissidents was Wei Jingsheng, and he came from precisely the kind of background just described, but at the time of the dissident movement was working as an electrician at Peking Zoo. He believed that the Four Modernisations would fail unless China adopted what he called the Fifth Modernisation – democracy. Wei maintained that even less controversial areas of development such as science and technology would not develop unless scientists were given complete freedom to express themselves.

Initially Deng Xiaoping allowed Democracy Wall to flourish, as the views expressed coincided with his own wish to introduce economic reforms, and he allowed the writers on Democracy Wall to attack the conservatives in the leadership. But this increasingly vocal movement for political freedom caused anxiety, especially when it was clear that it was not confined to the capital. All over the country people were demanding political change and greater civil liberties. The movement coincided with demonstrations in Peking by thousands of protesting peasants, complaining about the poverty in which they lived and demanding that the government do something to lessen their misery. The dissidents associated themselves with the protests. When Deng Xiaoping returned from a visit to the United States early in 1979 he clamped down on the movement. By then he needed no urging from his peers, as he himself was under attack by the young scribes who were now calling openly for democracy and castigating Deng as oppressive.

In March 1979 Deng established what are known as the 'Four Cardinal Principles' which were to guide the development of China. These were adherence to the principles of Marxism-Leninism-Mao Zedong Thought, the supremacy of the Communist Party, the socialist path, and the continuation of the so-called 'people's democratic dictatorship'. But despite the wording of the fourth principle, democracy was definitely not on the agenda. Democracy Wall was scrubbed clean of posters and over the next two years the more vocal of the dissenters were tried and imprisoned, including Wei Jingsheng who was gaoled for fifteen years. Not, the Chinese hasten to assure us, because of his views on democracy but because he betrayed state secrets to a foreign journalist. Though what state secrets an electrician at Peking Zoo could know is open to question. There are reports that following years in solitary confinement, Wei has gone mad.

The past decade has been characterised by a series of political relaxations, followed by clamp-downs. In 1978, the more open atmosphere allowed people to write pro-democracy posters on a wall until the leadership decided that it had all gone too far. The next, though less serious manifestation of the trend was in 1983–84, when the conservatives in the leadership became appalled by what they saw as the slackening of moral standards; the passion for Western pop music, the cynicism of the young, and the increasingly critical literature which was being published. So the campaign against 'spiritual pollution' was born. However, when it spread from its intended target into more harmless areas such as the way people dressed or did their hair, Deng Xiaoping called a halt. He had allowed it to start, but when it was pointed out to him that it was causing shivers of apprehension both amongst the intellectuals, who feared that it was the forerunner of another Cultural Revolution, and amongst foreign businessmen, who wondered whether it was the precursor of another period of instability, Deng decided that it had to stop.

The next ground swell occurred at the end of 1986, and was potentially much more serious. Towards the end of the year students in Shanghai and other cities started demonstrating. Initially their complaints were about living conditions. The university food and accommodation was bad; the teaching was poor; there were too many petty rules; prices were rising too high But the unrest soon gathered momentum and took on a highly political flavour, with demands for democracy and political plurality. It was clear that the students did not always know exactly what that meant, but they knew that they wanted it. The authorities showed patience until the demonstrations spread to Peking, then they clamped down. Ringleaders were arrested, and some are still in prison.

The protests had serious repercussions. Three prominent intellectuals were dismissed from the Party, including Liu Binyan, who has been in political trouble, on and off, since the early 1940s. One academic, the now-famous astrophysicist, Fang Lizhi, was accused of inciting the students to demonstrate, although when I talked to him in Peking earlier this year he denied this. He was removed from his job as Vice-President of the University of Science and Technology in Anhui Province and moved to the Academy of Sciences in Peking, where the authorities could keep a closer eye on him. To this day the 'Chinese Sakharov' as he is inevitably known, is completely unrepentant and, until he sought refuge in the US Embassy in Peking in June 1989, continued to voice his beliefs. He says that Marxism's day is over, and believes that China should adopt the Western system of non-governmental interference in the economy and people's political lives. Fang believes that China needs democracy in the sense of the freedom to speak out. He is certainly not opposed to socialism, but advocates the type of welfare socialism typified by Sweden. However, despite reports to the contrary, he does not call for complete Westernisation of China's politics and culture, and looks instead to the free-market economies of Asia, such as South Korea and Singapore. Fang's views are abhorrent to many in the Chinese leadership, and in June he was branded a traitor and a warrant was issued for his arrest for 'counter-revolutionary activities'. But although the government disliked China's leading dissidents stating their views so publicly, until June 1989 it did not prevent them from doing so. Fang Lizhi was allowed to talk to the foreign press, and occasionally to attend scientific meetings outside China. Liu Binyan has recently spent a period at Harvard University and was due to return to China. However, recent events have ruled that out for the time being.

The student demonstrations in 1986 had serious

repercusions for the Party leadership, and they led to the forced resignation of the late General Secretary of the Party, Hu Yaobang. The more conservative members of the leadership had always disapproved of Hu Yaobang, and the military had stood out against the proposal that he might take over from Deng as Chairman of the Military Commission. They considered him irresponsible and volatile, with a history of off-the-cuff gaffes whilst travelling abroad. He was certainly unpredictable and had a tendency to shoot verbally from the hip. He was accused of allowing the students too much freedom and of failing to curb their excesses before it was too late. So Deng sacrificed him, and Zhao Ziyang took on the mantle of Acting General Secretary of the Party in addition to the Premiership.

Zhao Ziyang, successor to Hu Yaobang, was confirmed as General Secretary of the Party at its Thirteenth Congress in 1987. He was a committed reformer, and of the radical school. As mentioned earlier, he pioneered both urban and rural reform in Sichuan. First he worked as a Party leader in his home Province of Henan in central China, then in the 1950s, because of his experience in land reform, he was moved to the southernmost Province of Guangdong. Although Zhao was initially in favour of the Great Leap Forward, the failure of the 1960 harvest prompted him to restore the policy of private plots and the household contract system, policies which he duplicated when he moved to Sichuan in the late 1970s. During the Cultural Revolution Zhao was attacked by the Red Guards in Canton for precisely such 'revisionist' agricultural policies, and was paraded through the streets wearing a dunce's cap.

Zhao Ziyang was a self-assured and charismatic character, who favoured tinted spectacles, and well-cut cream-coloured suits. Those who met him during his travels abroad have been impressed by his statesmanlike behaviour. But the job of Party chief has always been a sensitive one, and Zhao made it clear that he would prefer to remain in the more 'hands-on' job of Premier. From the mid-1980s the reforms encountered very serious problems, and Zhao, as one of the leading architects, was a natural target of attack by the more conservative leaders. By the spring of 1989 his overall control of the economy had devolved to the more cautious Prime Minister Li Peng, and one of the Vice-Premiers Yao Yilin, also an experienced planning guru. In an attempt to protect his own position, Zhao was constrained to make speeches condemning the negative aspects of the reforms, such as corruption and runaway capital investment.

What the government feared most was that the problems stemming from the economic reforms would push the increasingly vocal and restless urban workers to join forces with the increasingly recalcitrant students and present a real threat to public order, and their fears were well-founded.

Before discussing the cataclysmic events of April–June 1989 it is necessary to examine the degree to which there had been any political reform at all to accompany the economic reform. The Chinese leadership had ruled out any possibility of a multi-Party state, but they were redefining the way forward. By 1979 Zhao Ziyang had already said that belief in a planned economy was not an essential part of a commitment to socialism. In 1984 a commentary in the *People's Daily* made the startling statement that 'Marxism-Leninism cannot solve our problems'. (This was quickly amended to 'cannot solve all our problems', but the dyke had been breached.) Young economists argued that Marxism did not rule out private ownership. At the Thirteenth Party Congress in 1987 Zhao Ziyang caused ideological consternation by restating the view, which had been gaining currency for some time, that China is 'in the initial stage of socialism', and would remain so for a very long time. In essence this meant that China was abandoning a commitment to becoming a Communist state in the foreseeable future. It was a fudge, as it meant that China could continue to call itself socialist, whilst toying with some of the features of capitalism.

The leadership decreed that there was to be increasing separation of the Party apparatus from that of the state, and this tied in with the economic reforms. It meant that in factories, at least in theory, the members of the Party Committees were to concern themselves solely with ideological matters, and not interfere in the management of the factory. But in a socialist society the dividing line is often very blurred, and there still continued to be interference by the Party. However, the new policy nibbled at the edges of the absolute power of the Party, and so incurred the resentment of many apparatchiks.

A degree of democracy was introduced into local politics. At county level (there are some 2000 counties in China) there were multi-candidate elections for governing committees. One could argue that this was true democracy, as the candidates were, in theory, chosen because of their abilities and not because of political affiliation. However, it was difficult, although not impossible, for anyone to be elected if he or she was actively opposed to the Communist Party. At one local election in Peking, for a district which included most of the universities, a large number of people crossed out the names of all the candidates, and instead wrote in the name of the dissident Fang Lizhi!

In 1988 Zhao Ziyang had started to introduce multi-candidate elections for posts such as deputy provincial governor or mayor. Naturally, those who lost out were less than contented with such moves towards political reform.

The increasingly strong voice of China's parliament, the National People's Congress, was another sign of a degree of political liberalisation. At a full meeting of the NPC in 1988 there was extremely lively and open debate, and the NPC exercised its power to reject and amend new laws. However, in the spring of 1989, with newly-imposed government controls over the economy, the NPC's meeting was a much more muted affair.

These moves towards a loosening of the Party's stranglehold, although to be applauded, were wholly inadequate. They fell far short of the political developments in the Soviet Union and some other countries in the Eastern Bloc. The delegates to the NPC are not chosen by direct election, and in 1987 Deng Xiaoping told a Western leader that although China was moving towards democracy, it would take a very long time before it attained it. He said that the vast majority of people in China were not educated enough to be given universal franchise (which, one could argue, is a severe indictment of forty years of a Communist education system) and that if they were to be given it, there would be anarchy.

These so-called political reforms may have been a beginning, but one thing was certain – the Chinese Communist Party was not going to let go of its monopoly of power. The Eight Democratic Parties, often cited as providing a voice of opposition, only boast a few thousand members, against the

48 million of the Chinese Communist Party. However over the years, there has been growing disillusionment with the Communist Party, with its corruption and increasing ideological bankruptcy. And now, apart from those people who join the Party for political advancement, many people scoff at the idea of applying for membership.

I travelled widely in China in March and April 1989, and I now look back on it as a halcyon period. I have never experienced such openness in China. People from all walks of life were prepared to speak quite openly about the problems which the country was encountering. They grumbled about corruption, rising prices, inflation, nepotism, crime, the lack of attention to the education system. I found that people were most amenable to being interviewed. I could ring up a complete stranger, or drop in at his office, and be welcomed. Girls on switchboards would spend fifteen minutes trying to track someone down (girls on Chinese switchboards generally have a formidable reputation for rudeness). Even Party cadres told me political jokes. Such openness was most welcome, but it was also an indication of an extreme social malaise.

To my amazement I found that people referred back to Mao Zedong's day with something approaching nostalgia. And these were people who had suffered horribly in the Cultural Revolution. An elderly professor said to me that although there had been bad things in Mao's day, at least there was little crime or corruption, no inflation and stable prices. He concluded by saying 'Surely that's what socialism is all about'. However, in the next breath he went on to talk about the importance of China forging ahead to become a major economic power, so demonstrating an inadequate grasp of the contradictions of his position.

It became quite clear that 'democracy' was much talked about, at least by the urban population. It was equally clear that people were not too sure what it was. A young worker explained it to me as 'Firstly, freedom of the press'. And secondly? He replied, with an engaging grin 'I haven't got that far yet'. I found a great deal of cynicism about the leadership, with people saying that it did not matter who was at the top, as they were all equally bad. When I asked why they did not do something about it instead of just grumbling, the intellectuals said that they did not have the courage to put actions to words.

THE CHINESE PEOPLE STAND UP

As one of them said, 'We've had the guts knocked out of us'. Yet within a matter of weeks China's young intellectuals had changed the face of China.

THE TIANANMEN SQUARE MASSACRE

On 15 April 1989 the former General Secretary of the CCP, Hu Yaobang, who had been forced to resign in January 1987 following student unrest, died. It is said that he had a heart attack at a meeting of the Politburo (on which he still had a seat) following an argument over the future of the reforms. His death gave rise to large-scale student demonstrations in Peking. The students mourned Hu as a liberal and a champion of the reforms. He was certainly the latter, although there is little justification for the former appellation. However, the man was certainly open-minded and was himself always a fountain of new ideas. But whatever he had been in life, in death he became an icon for the students.

Tens of thousands of students from the campuses of the capital marched to the centre of the city. They massed outside the Great Hall of the People on the west side of Tiananmen Square, in front of the gates of Zhongnanhai where China's leaders live, on the north-west side of the square, and in the centre of the square itself.They shouted 'Down with tyranny, up with democracy' and demanded freedom of the press, an end to corruption, and that the assets of the children of the top leaders should be open to public scrutiny. They also demanded a dialogue with General Secretary of the Party, Zhao Ziyang and the Prime Minister Li Peng.

The government issued stern warnings to the students to stop their demonstrations, but their words fell on deaf ears. The demonstrations grew in size until the funeral ceremony for Hu Yaobang ten days later. It was relayed by loudspeaker to the tens of thousands of demonstrators in the square. Zhao Ziyang delivered the eulogy, omitting to mention that Hu Yaobang had been forced to resign. As expected, the demonstrations continued in the run-up to 4 May. This marked the seventieth anniversary of the 4 May 1919 Movement. Then, there had been a great student protest at the provisions of the Treaty of Versailles, which transferred a part of Chinese territory from the defeated Germans to the Japanese. The movement widened to attack the weak and corrupt Chinese government, and eventually helped to overthrow the old order. Some of China's aged leaders had been active in the movement, and they must have shuddered when they saw the new wave of student demonstrations, and wondered if this presaged the toppling of their order.

Although the leaders agreed to talk to some of the the students, they refused to talk to representatives of the unofficial students unions, so the talks were doomed from the start. By now the youthful demonstrators had the support of the citizens of Peking, including workers, professional people, journalists and even some Party members and policemen. It was an extraordinary indictment of the Chinese Communist Party's leadership. And still the leadership did nothing. One question still being asked is why did they not do something to defuse the situation before it had reached uncontrollable proportions? We shall probably never know the answer. However, there is more than one likely explanation. The most obvious is that the Chinese leadership was full of men who had never been answerable to their own people throughout their many years, in some cases decades, at the top. They were used to dictating what the people should do, and expected that once again 'the masses' would be cowed by the voice of authority. What they had clearly not understood was that they were dealing with a new breed of young Chinese, whose spirit had not been crushed by a succession of political campaigns. They were the new elite, the tiny percentage of the population who have had the privilege of a tertiary education, and will subsequently have the chance of a good job, or a period of study abroad. Many are the children of high-ranking Party or state cadres, and have all the assurance of any country's gilded youth.

Another very likely explanation for the inaction is that the leadership was divided on how to respond. Indeed, we know that there was sharp disagreement over a very hard-line commentary in the *People's Daily* on 26 April. Zhao Ziyang had been on a visit to North Korea at the time, and on his return voiced his disagreement on the wording of the piece. This further exacerbated the split between the more liberal members of the Politburo, led by Zhao, and the conservative element led by Deng Xiaoping and Li Peng. Deng had already made it clear that he wanted the protests crushed 'by any means', although it was still some weeks before that was to happen.

A third reason for the leaders' inaction was the impending visit by President Gorbachev for the first Sino-Soviet Summit for thirty years. Although the student demonstrations were a colossal embarrassment to the Chinese leaders, their violent suppression just before the visit of the man who correctly or incorrectly has become a byword for liberalism in a communist state, would have been bad propaganda. The demonstrations caused total disruption to the highly significant visit, and Mr Gorbachev's programme was constantly having to be rearranged because of the numbers of demonstrators in Peking. The Chinese leadership was enraged by the huge loss of face.

Meanwhile some 3000 students had gone on hunger strike under the hot May skies, and medical staff were in constant attendance. After the Summit Zhao Ziyang and Li Peng visited the hunger strikers. Zhao Ziyang was tearful and clearly shaken, and apologised for not having visited them sooner. His behaviour infuriated the hardline Politburo members. Some of the student leaders were granted the meeting which they had demanded with Li Peng, who was by then the students' main target. The discussions broke up almost before they started, when he refused the students' demand for a televised debate.

Meanwhile, the unrest had spread to many cities around the country, with people protesting in their thousands. In some cases the demonstrations, which did not necessarily only involve students, led to violence and destruction.

President Gorbachev left Peking on 18 May, and at around midnight on the 19th loudspeakers around Tiananmen Square crackled into life and announced that martial law had been declared. At a press conference, a very self-assured Li Peng declared that the authorities had had no choice but to act, and he was backed up by the octogenarian President of China Yang Shangkun. The people held their breath as they waited for the troops to move in. Amd move in they did, in their tens of thousands. But the people in the centre of the city numbered hundreds of thousands, and they ignored the orders to disperse. Instead, they blocked the passage of the army vehicles. They talked to the soldiers and explained why they were protesting. They said that they were not counter-revolutionaries trying to overthrow the Party and the state, but were merely asking for more democracy and less corruption.

Many of the soldiers were clearly nonplussed, and some expressed sympathy for the protesters. There was little violence, and some of the troops withdrew. It must have been one of the most peaceful impositions of martial law that the world has ever known.

For several days there was a stalemate. A number of students kept up their hunger strike, and were rushed to hospital and put on drips when they collapsed with exhaustion and dehydration. Numbers in the square fluctuated, although many people arrived from the provinces to join in the protests. The attention of the world's media was focused on the extraordinary events. Then the students from some of the art colleges constructed a 30-foot-high polystyrene figure modelled on the Statue of Liberty. They called it the Goddess of Democracy and assembled it in the square directly in front of Mao Zedong's Mausoleum, next to the Martyrs' Monument, and facing Mao's portrait on Tiananmen. The students said that they had given the Goddess Western features because there was no democracy in China. The statue was a breath-taking affront to the Chinese leadership.

On 2 June another contingent of troops tried to make its way into the centre of Peking. They were mostly very young, and were unarmed except for truncheons. They seemed to have little idea of what to do, and when the crowds harangued them, emptied out their knapsacks and debagged some of them, a few burst into tears. They retreated in disorder. It is impossible to say why the PLA carried out such a fruitless exercise. One explanation is that the leaders wanted to lull the protesters into a false sense of security. However, no army commander would ever agree to subject his troops to ridicule by crowds of civilians.

By then it was clear that at least one army commander, the Commander of the 38th Army of the Peking Military Region, was unhappy at the imposition of martial law, and was not prepared to use his troops against the people. It was said that he himself had a daughter at university in the city, and many more of his troops would have had friends and relatives demonstrating in the square. However it was known that the commanders of at least six out of the seven Military Regions had sent letters to the Politburo supporting the move. Of course, had they not supported it they would have been labelled counter-revolutionaries.

Even on Saturday 3 June people in the square were saying that the People's Liberation Army was the army of the people and would never harm them. A few hours later they were proved to have been tragically wrong. In the early hours of the morning on Sunday 4 June tanks and Armoured Personnel Carriers moved into the centre of Peking and entered Tiananmen Square. Although some attempts were made to move the crowd out of the square, these attempts were perfunctory. Furthermore, no one expected anything appalling to happen, and so did not move. The square was still crammed with tens of thousands of people. There were young students of both sexes, workers, people from all walks of life both from Peking and the provinces. There were even young children.

Students and other protesters linked hands and pleaded with the troops to halt and not to shoot. Chinese and foreign witnesses watched with disbelief as the troops gunned down unarmed protesters and ran their tanks and APCs over hunger strikers lying in their tents and any other protesters who got in their way. The crowd was enraged and set fire to one APC which was stranded on a barrier. Other vehicles were set on fire. Although the students managed to protect some soldiers from the wrath of the crowd, a number were lynched and mutilated and their bodies were burnt.

There was total mayhem, with bodies littering the ground in and around the square. Flames rose into the sky, illuminating the carnage. The People's Army had turned on the people. There was rage, grief and disbelief that such a thing could have happened. People around the world watched with growing horror as it became clear that the government of a country which had seemed to be opening up to liberal ideas had behaved with a barbarity unprecedented in recent history. The condemnation was universal.

For the time being, the protest movement was over. The people of Peking were left to count their dead. This was no easy task, for the dead and injured were scattered around the hospitals of the capital. Over the ensuing days terrible rumours started that the army had used flame-throwers to incinerate piles of corpses, to hide the full extent of the massacre. We shall probably never know how many died, but eye-witness estimates range from 700 to 3000. In October 1949 Mao Zedong looked out over Tiananmen Square and said, 'The Chinese people have stood up.' Forty years later the Chinese people once again stood up, this time against Mao's successor Deng Xiaoping, only to be massacred by the Chinese People's Liberation Army.

The rumours spread. There was disaffection amongst the troops, there were battles between the 38th Army, which had refused to move against the protesters, and the 27th Army which had massacred them. Troops loyal to the protesters were moving on Peking. Other troops were moving in to support the hardline leaders. There would be civil war. In the event, despite the sound of sporadic gunfire around the city, the army held together.

There was violence in many cities around China, with vehicles set on fire and reports of brutal killings by the army and the People's Armed Police. But nowhere could compare with Peking. The Mayor of Shanghai defused a mass demonstration by saying that no troops would enter the city, and he called on workers' groups to enforce law and order themselves. This was a highly successful move, but it came after demonstrators had set fire to a train that had killed a number of protesters sitting in its path.

And now the government started one of the most complete disinformation campaigns in the history of the Chinese Communist Party. With breathtaking cynicism they had clearly decided that if they were going to lie it might as well be a colossal lie. Doctoring news footage of the events of 4 June, they initially announced that only a handful of civilians had been killed in the square, (and those by accident) whilst, on the contrary, armed protesters had murdered some 1000 or so innocent and heroic soldiers. They cut the news film to show demonstrators setting fire to army vehicles. Over and over again they showed the mutilated and blackened corpses of the soldiers who had been lynched. Not one picture was shown of the corpses scattered on the ground following the bursts of machine-gun fire. They did not show the pictures of tangled corpses and their bicycles which had appeared on the front pages of almost every newspaper in the West. The weeping mothers of dead soldiers were shown on television time and time again, but not the weeping mothers of the student protesters.

Li Peng appeared in public to give a triumphant salute to the troops who had crushed the demonstrators and to congratulate them on having suppressed a counter-revolutionary movement. When Deng Xiaoping finally reappeared after a three-week absence, flanked by a number of hardline octogenarians, his message was the same. The People's Liberation Army, full of love for the people, had saved the nation, the party and the government from a counter-revolution.

Although many people around China already know the truth about the massacre in Tiananmen Square, and the word will filter through in time, there are many who will not have heard foreign radio stations, and will be only too inclined to believe the government's version of events. After all, how could the People's Army have turned on the people?

And then the reign of terror started. Warrants were issued for the arrest of the student leaders and many others, accused of violence, destroying public property or engaging in counter-revolutionary activities. Suspects were searched and arrested at railway stations. Those who could went into hiding or even fled the country. Soon a number of people were tried and condemned to death. The authorities had no hesitation in showing that the accused had been beaten. They were bruised and cowed, and were shown being interrogated at gun-point. Chillingly, some had been identified from foreign newsfilm. People were exhorted to turn in friends and relatives. A Stalinist reign of terror had begun. During previous political campaigns the people were egged on against their fellow citizens, and during the Cultural Revolution the Red Guards were used as the scourge. But this time the full panoply of a police state was brought to bear on the population.

The government did not hesitate to demonstrate that it had used secret cameras to identify the leaders of the protest. It claimed that Taiwanese *agents provocateurs* had incited the protesters. It tried to discredit student leaders like Wu'er Kaixi by showing him enjoying a banquet whilst fellow protesters were on hunger strike. The aim was to intimidate the population, a sure sign that the government is only too well aware of the huge public resentment against it, and knows that it can no longer rely on the co-operation of the people of China.

At the time of writing, the beginning of July 1989, some 2000 people had been arrested, and about 20 executed by a bullet in the back of the head. It should be noted, that for the time being at least, the majority of victims have been workers rather than students, although there is no doubt that a number of students will end up in prison and labour-reform camps. But the Chinese government has consistently taken the line that the majority of the students were manipulated innocents, who did not know what they were doing, and were being influenced by a 'handful of bad people'. The government probably also realised that there would be greater public sympathy for students who had merely called for an end to corruption and for greater political freedom, than for workers and others who had been seen to set fire to buses and generally contribute to violent disorder.

Another factor may be that the workers have much greater potential to cause social and economic disorder than the students have. They have the power to paralyse the economy by go-slows and strikes, although they may be reluctant to try the latter tactic given the present hardline control. But the government has always been more afraid of the workers than the students, and with good reason, for there are some 70 million of them. The orthodox Marxists in the leadership will remember that a true revolution is based on an urban proletariat, and will be determined not to let such a revolution happen.

The world has, quite properly, reacted with horror and condemnation to the arbitrary arrests and executions. But some people, myself included, would say that it is high time that the world woke up to China's appalling record on human rights. Each year thousands of people in China are executed for a variety of crimes, ranging from robbery with violence, rape, hooliganism and murder to the catch-all 'counter-revolutionary crimes'. Rarely does one hear any condemnation of the Chinese for this large number of judicial killings. Perhaps now people will realise that the Chinese should be subjected to the same close scrutiny as any of the other more notorious flouters of human rights like Romania, El Salvador or South Africa. And the supreme irony is that the USSR, so often flagellated on the question of human rights, has for decades had a better record than China. For too long the world has only seen the rational and public face of Deng Xiaoping's reformist China. But for all the good which undoubtedly was achieved in the early years of the reforms, the system itself was unchanged. It remains repressive, totalitarian, monolithic and ruthless. The contempt of the Chinese leaders for their people is breathtaking in its scale, and is quite as monumental as that of their predecessor, Mao Zedong.

Although it is too soon after the massacre to be able to assess it objectively, some questions have to be asked and answers attempted. Was the tragedy inevitable? Who ordered the massacre? How widespread was the student unrest, and is it fair to call it counter-revolutionary? What is the situation now?

For all the reasons listed earlier in this chapter, I believe that some sort of social disorder was inevitable. There was growing discontent in many sectors of society. The economic reforms and the opening upto the outside world had brought a degree of freedom which had greatly diminished the fear that gripped China during the darkest years of the Maoist era, those who had studied abroad came back imbued with new ideas about the rights of the human being in contemporary society, technological progress meant that people had better access to foreign radio stations, and improved communications within China itself made it much easier for ideas to spread from city to city. The democracy movement even made most effective use of that tool of modern communication – the fax machine.

Was it inevitable that hundreds, possibly even thousands of unarmed protesters, bystanders and soldiers had to be killed? Of course it was not. Any method of crowd control is brutal, whether it is tear gas, water cannon or rubber bullets. But all those would have been preferable to live ammunition and the crushing tracks and wheels of tanks and APCs. The Chinese have the standard equipment used to control crowds in the West. They chose not to use it. This means that they deliberately terrorised the population with the most brutal means possible. And in doing so they were also sending a clear message to Zhao Ziyang and those of his supporters who might have contemplated any sort of counter-movement – the demonstrations would be crushed at whatever cost.

Who was responsible? Probably most of the hard-line leaders who are now in power in China concurred with the decision, but the primary blame must lie with Deng Xiaoping, President Yang Shangkun, Prime Minister Li Peng and probably also the man in charge of public security and the law, Qiao Shi. Why did they do it? Deng and Li, together with such men as Chen Yun and Peng Zhen, have been in or near the top leadership for at least half a century. Their policies over the decades may have been pragmatic to a greater or lesser degree, but they never intended to concede power as long as they were alive. Suddenly they were challenged by thousands of young, brash, fearless students. These in turn were joined by intellectuals who were thought to have had all the spirit crushed out of them. And they were also supported by a potentially disruptive urban workforce. Deng and the others must have remembered their own power as young student agitators, and the fact that they themselves managed to overthrow the old order. But no one who has had such power for so long is going to concede willingly that he, like an old Emperor has, in his turn, lost the Mandate of Heaven. Instead, he accuses the agitators of trying to overthrow the Party, and the state rounds them up, imprisons them, executes a number of them, and reasserts an uneasy control over a silent and resentful population.

Were the demonstrators counter-revolutionaries? The definition in the Chinese legal code is short and vague, but it boils down to the fact that anyone who seeks to subvert or overthrow the state is a counter-revolutionary. When the students started the protests their demands were, as stated earlier, press freedom (and the number of journalists who supported them showed that the practitioners themselves wanted a freer hand), an end to corruption, and more democracy. They hastened to say that they were not against the Communist Party, nor did they seek its overthrow. They simply wanted a leadership which was unsullied by corruption, and which was not 'divorced from the masses'. However, as the protests went on, the students became very specific in their demands that certain leaders should resign. Gradually, as the students saw that the leadership was showing no sign of acceding to even their most basic requests, they hardened their attitude. And by the time the troops moved in to crush the protests it is probably true to say that the students had moved from criticism of specific aspects of the system to a criticism of the entire system. Some students were even advocating a wholesale change of the established order. In the eyes of the present Chinese leadership this made them appear counter-revolutionaries.

A question crucial to the future of the democratic movement and indeed to the future of China is, how widespread and well organised was the student movement? The general consensus is that it was very small, and even in Peking itself it was less than totally cohesive. It was weeks before a certain number of student leaders emerged, and the students' demands were vague and uncoordinated. It is also agreed, even by the students themselves, that their own behaviour was often dictatorial and undemocratic. Strategically however, the Peking campaign was well co-ordinated. The students blocked streets and erected barricades with a clear set of orders. There was very little violence, and everyone who talked to the students found them persuasive, orderly and determined, but for the most part politically naive. They were not very sure what they wanted, but were absolutely sure of what they didn't want.

Although there were widespread student demonstrations throughout the country, it is difficult to know how well co-ordinated these were, or whether they largely sprang up as a response to the movement in Peking. There is little or no evidence that groups of like-minded individuals from all walks of life have been emerging all over China to discuss its political future. The concerns of most people have been of a practical rather than an ideological nature. But this is changing.

One cannot discuss the events of the Tiananmen Massacre without closely examining the role of the Chinese People's Liberation Army, the PLA. Before the troops moved in to crush the demonstrators, there was an enormous amount of discussion both in China and abroad as to whether the PLA would follow the imposition of martial law by moving against the people in the square. Opinions varied. Most thought that they would not. Some thought that certain units might, whilst others definitely would not. It was argued that some regional commanders would be loyal to Deng Xiaoping and others would not. In the end the People's Army did as many armies have done before. It obeyed orders, and showed that it was not the army of the people, but the army of the Chinese Communist Party, of which the majority of soldiers are members.

There is no doubt that the troops had been heavily indoctrinated and told that they were saving China from a counter-revolutionary movement. However, the moment they entered the square it must have been clear to them that their foe consisted of unarmed citizens, many of whom were very young indeed. There can be no excuse for their brutality. What happened on 3–4 June 1989 will forever change the reputation of the PLA as the 'People's Army'. Its relationship with the people of China will never be the same again.

At the time of writing the authorities in Peking had already announced major changes in the CCP. Although Zhao Ziyang had clearly been ousted from his post as General Secretary of the Party at around the time martial law was declared, it was 24 June before the name of the new General Secretary was announced. It is Jiang Zemin, former Mayor and subsequently Party Secretary of the city of Shanghai, and a protégé of Deng Xiaoping. The current composition of the six-man Politburo Standing Committee is a clear signal that the economic reforms will continue at a controlled pace and that democratic reform will not continue at all.

Before leaving the subject of these recent events, one must try to assess the extent of this tragedy in the light of China's recent turbulent history. The Tiananmen Square massacre was an appalling and unforgivable event. But compared with the tens of thousands who died during the Cultural Revolution it was limited in its scale. One could argue that Mao Zedong has more to answer for than Deng Xiaoping in having cynically launched ordinary Chinese against each other in mayhem and bloodshed, as happened in the Cultural Revolution. However, the Cultural Revolution happened twenty years ago. Then, many in the West were reluctant to believe that what they had seen as Mao's utopian dream of a truly egalitarian society had brought such catastrophe in its wake. But since that time the world and China have moved on. China has had increasing contact with the outside world and is a member of the United Nations Security Council. The atrocities which people were reluctant to believe had happened in the 1960s are even less acceptable in the 1980s.

CHAPTER SIX

CHINA'S PLACE IN THE WORLD

China's leaders claim that their foreign policy over the past four decades has been consistent. If one accepts that the foreign policy concerns of China are those of any other country – to secure its borders and preserve its sovereignty – then their claim is true. But changes in Chinese foreign policy have led to dramatic changes in its major alliances. Put simply, the Chinese were closely allied with the Soviet Union in the 1950s; during the 1960s they were hostile towards both the Soviet Union and the United States; in the 1970s the Soviet Union was still the arch-enemy and China considered an alliance with the United States a useful safeguard against its northern neighbour; and in the 1980s there has been a dramatic diminution of hostility towards the Soviet Union, leading to normalisation of relations after a break of nearly three decades. Now, although China still declares itself part of the Third World, its foreign policy is closely allied with its desire for economic expansion. Gone are the days when relations with fraternal Communist parties were the linchpin of foreign policy. Now state-to-state relations are of far greater importance.

When the Communists took power in China in October 1949 it seemed natural that they would ally with the world's leading socialist power, the Soviet Union. There had been close contacts between the two Communist parties since the 1920s. Mao, for all his heterodoxy, still viewed the Soviet Union as the fountainhead of Marxist ideology, and despite the friction between the two fraternal parties over the years, they were natural allies. Furthermore, Mao Zedong's new government needed a great deal of economic assistance. The country had been ravaged by decades of war, industry needed to be revitalised and large numbers of new industrial plants had to be built. To achieve this China needed huge, favourable loans and technical assistance, and the Soviet Union was a potential source of such aid.

Mao did not take the Soviet option without due consideration. There were indications during 1948 and until the summer of 1949 that Mao was interested in having some sort of relationship with the United States. On more than one occasion Mao made it clear that his government would be willing to have relations with any country which would respect China's territorial integrity and would agree not to give any more aid to Chiang Kai-shek's Nationalist government. Throughout the spring and early summer of 1949 the Communists were in contact with the United States' Ambassador to China, John Leighton Stuart. They invited him to Peking (he was resident in Nanjing), but when he delayed in accepting, the Communists began to realise that the precondition for United States' recognition would be a promise on the Chinese part not to ally with the Soviet Union. Since China needed economic assistance, and had no guarantee that the Americans would give aid as well as recognition, this was too high a price to pay.

On 1 July 1949 John Leighton Stuart received instructions not to negotiate with the Communists, and on the very same day Mao's famous essay *On the People's Democratic Dictatorship* was published. This stated that China would have to 'lean to one side', and that side was to be the Soviet Union. It has often been argued that it would not have made any difference whether the United States' Ambassador had received different instructions from his government, as Mao had already made up his mind with whom he was going to ally. I am not sure that that is so. It is more likely that the lukewarm American response pushed him in the direction of the Soviet Union. It is also likely that the United States would have been extremely surprised and even embarrassed had China forfeited its relationship with the USSR for the sake of recognition by the United States. At that time the Americans were strongly anti-Communist, and Secretary of State Dean Acheson was most concerned about 'the spread of totalitarian communism in Asia'. Acheson also believed that the Chinese Communists did not place much importance on recognition by the United States, whilst such recognition would cause considerable alarm amongst other Asian countries.

So in December 1949 Mao Zedong himself led a delegation to Moscow to negotiate a new treaty with the Russians. By all accounts it was a very odd visit (Mao's first trip abroad, incidentally) as Stalin was apparently cool towards his largest socialist ally. Mao and a small group of advisers were in Moscow for two months, and it is still unclear what they were doing throughout the period. One thing which is clear, though, is that there was some very hard bargaining. Zhou Enlai and other Chinese leaders did not arrive in Moscow until February, when the treaty was ready to be signed. Mao later said that Stalin had initially not been willing to sign a treaty, but finally it was agreed. Neither side was happy with the end result, and Mao later described the process as 'like snatching meat from the mouth of a tiger'. The Russians felt that the US $300 million which they were offering to the Chinese at 1 per cent interest rate over five years was more than generous, given the state of their own ruined economy after the Second World War. The Chinese felt that it was far from generous, and indeed it was less than the Russians had granted to the Poles. Furthermore, it was to be paid in roubles (old) which were promptly devalued, leaving the Chinese with 25 per cent less in actual value than had been promised.

This Sino-Soviet Treaty of Friendship, Alliance and Mutual Assistance was very similar to that which the Russians and the Nationalists had signed in 1945, and it contained several provisions which had a distinctly colonial flavour. The Russians were to use Port Arthur (now Dalian) as a naval base; there was to be joint ownership of the Chinese Eastern and South Manchurian Railway (later known as the Chinese Changchun Railway) and there were to be joint stock companies to exploit oil and non-ferrous metal mining in the north-west Province of Xinjiang. Although the conditions which the Russians exacted were supposed to last only until 1952, Mao must have wondered whether China had shaken off one set of foreign hands only to fall into another. In return for the concessions, however, the Chinese got their loan, and an agreement that if either state were to be attacked by Japan or any state allied to it (presumably the United States) then the other would go to its defence. It is worth noting that when, on 1 October 1949, Zhou Enlai invited all foreign countries to establish relations with China on the basis of equality, mutual benefit and mutual respect for territory and sovereignty, the Soviet Union did not explicitly say that it accepted those principles. Other countries, including Britain, explicitly did accept them.

The ideological strains between the two countries had not diminished. Although Mao still believed that the Soviet Union led the world Communist movement, he also felt that China had something to offer as a revolutionary alternative, 'The Way of Mao Zedong'. Liu Shaoqi articulated this as a Chinese or Asiatic form of Marxism, particularly applicable to those societies similar to China's – backward, semi-colonial and agricultural. The Soviet Union, although it had shown little interest in revolutionary movements in Asia, took a dim view of China setting itself up as a model for such movements. Mao Zedong had already articulated the concept of what , much later, came to be known as the 'intermediate zone'. This described a world with the Soviet Union at one end and the United States at the other. In between the two giants was a whole host of countries, particularly in Africa, Asia and Latin America, which were colonial or semi-colonial, and which were all struggling for their freedom – this was the 'intermediate zone' . Mao believed that those countries were ripe for revolution. He also believed that such revolution could only come about by violent means, and this was to become another source of contention between Mao and the next leader of the Soviet Union, Nikita Krushchev.

But before such ideological differences were eventually to destroy relations between China and the Soviet Union, China was plunged into the Korean War. Hostilities broke out on 25 June 1950, and at first the Chinese had no reason to suppose that they would be drawn into it. Although it has been argued by cold war warriors that China had intended from the first to join the war, this does not accord with the fact that Mao had already ordered partial demobilisation, and the Chinese leaders were much occupied with the problems of land reform. The last thing Mao wanted was a war. The Communists had been fighting for over twenty years, and they now wanted to breathe life back into their moribund country. But it gradually became clear that Kim Il Sung's North Korean troops were not going to have an easy victory, and that the South Korean and United Nations' forces were gaining ground. The Chinese warned the United Nations that China could not hold back if troops invaded North Korean territory. A Chinese general was invited to the United Nations to discuss the possibility of establishing a buffer zone south of the Yalu River, but on the very day of his arrival the American Commander in South Korea, General George MacArthur, launched an assault northwards towards the border between Manchuria and North Korea. On China's National Day, 1 October 1950, Mao announced that Chinese troops would be sent in under the name of the Chinese People's Volunteers. There is evidence that the decision was taken by Mao and a only a handful of other leaders and that many of the leaders were against it. Mao apparently agonised over the decision for two or three days. He knew that there was a real chance that the Chinese troops would be defeated, for this time they were fighting the armed might of the United States.

China suffered terrible losses in the Korean War, both in men and in money. Much has been made of the 'human wave' tactics used by the CPV, and it was said that it showed how little the Chinese leaders cared about the lives of their soldiers. There is no doubt that such tactics were used on occasion, but the official history of the US Marine Corps gives another side of the picture. It says that far from using mass attack as their main strategy the Chinese generally attacked in small numbers, emerged as if from nowhere, and faded without trace. In other words they used the classic guerrilla tactics which they had employed against the Japanese and the KMT troops.

The Soviet Union was determined at all costs not to engage in direct confrontation with the United States, but was willing to provide China with the weaponry to act as its proxy. Even that was in short supply, and only when the war had reached a stalemate in the summer of 1951 did the USSR supply a sufficient quantity of *matériel*, and they made the Chinese pay for every item. China borrowed US $1.4 billion in the years after 1950, and over half of that was to pay off the debt they had incurred with the Soviet Union. Mao had come to realise that there was no such thing as a free ally. Furthermore,

China was now branded an aggressor by the United States, which had contemplated carrying the war into Chinese territory and had even mooted the idea of a nuclear attack against China. The Korean War forced China even further into the Soviet camp, which the Russians had, no doubt, foreseen. But another important result of the war was that it made the United States resolved to continue support for Chiang Kai-shek's government in Taiwan. Prior to the Korean War the United States' administration had concluded that the Kuomintang government was by then a toothless mastiff.

After the Korean armistice was agreed in July 1953 China could once again concentrate on the task of national reconstruction. China's leaders were faced with the dilemma which has always determined the country's foreign policy. Should it aim for autonomy, but then be faced with a very slow pace of development because of lack of foreign credit and technology? Or should it accept aid, and then inevitably be beholden to the donor? In the early and mid-1950s China opted for the latter course. From 1950 the Soviet Union had numbers of advisers in Chinese ministries, especially the Ministry of Defence, and a large number of Russian technicians were working in China, particularly in the industrial North-East. Between 1950 and 1957 the Soviet Union gave China a total of 8.1 billion roubles (old) to help build industrial plant. Mao admitted that the Chinese had no idea how to go about reconstruction, and acknowledged the enormous help given by this huge transfer of technology.

Stalin died in March 1953, and Nikita Krushchev brought in a new era. As stated earlier, Mao admired Stalin, but was also critical of the fact that Stalin established a dictatorship which brooked no criticism. There is considerable irony in this, as Mao was similarly culpable in the ensuing years. Mao and Krushchev never enjoyed the uneasy bond that Mao had had with Stalin, but Krushchev started a series of visits to China over the next five years, and Mao again visited the Soviet Union. Stalin had never visited China, and during Krushchev's visit to China with Bulganin to celebrate the fifth anniversary of the People's Republic many of the clauses of the 1950 Treaty of Friendship were abrogated, and the joint stock company in Xinjiang was acknowledged as a clear case of exploitation of the Chinese. Port Arthur was also handed back, two years later than initially agreed. A new loan was agreed, as well as aid for more industrial projects. At last it seemed as if the relationship might be moving on to a more equal plane.

In 1954 China began to emerge on to the world stage. Zhou Enlai had a meeting with Jawaharlal Nehru in June that year, and advocated a relationship based on the Five Principles of Peaceful Coexistence, and these remain the touchstone of foreign policy at the present time. These were: mutual respect for each other's territorial integrity and sovereignty; non-aggression; non-interference in each other's internal affairs; equality and mutual benefit; and peaceful coexistence. These principles were by no means always adhered to in the years ahead, but they were a good starting point. The Five Principles had first been articulated in 1954 when India gave up the extraterritorial privileges in Tibet which it had inherited from the British, and the question of Tibet will be discussed later in this chapter.

From April to July 1954 the Geneva Conference was held to thrash out the problems of Korea and Indo-China, and the urbane Zhou Enlai made a very favourable impression. It was at the Geneva Conference that Zhou offered his hand to the then US Secretary of State, John Foster Dulles, who was viscerally anti-Communist. Dulles refused to shake it, which swung opinion even further in Zhou's favour.

During 1954 and 1955 Peaceful Coexistence was the catch-phrase, and was also known as the Bandung Line. This name was taken from the Afro-Asian meeting held in Bandung in Indonesia in April 1955, which stressed that all the countries of Asia had the right to peace and independence. This meeting laid the ground for visits to Peking by several Asian leaders and an extensive visit to Africa by Zhou Enlai. That same year Zhou suggested that there should be regular discussions with the United States. These started in Geneva in 1955. They were later transferred to Warsaw and, with occasional interruptions, they remained the basis for Sino-US relations until they moved on to a much higher plane in 1971.

The relatively even tempo of Sino-Soviet relations received a jolt in February 1956 when Krushchev used the platform of the Twentieth Congress of the Communist Party of the Soviet Union to attack the memory of Stalin in a secret speech. Mao

Zedong was angry that China had neither been consulted nor forewarned that this was to happen, and in spite of his reservations about Stalin he still felt that such criticism was completely unacceptable. But that was not the only cause for irritation, in Chinese eyes. At the same meeting Krushchev revised one of the basic tenets of Leninism – the inevitability of war. He stated that, under certain conditions, it was possible for a Communist party to take power without a violent revolution. Mao himself adhered rigidly to the idea that the international situation made war inevitable, and that a Communist party could achieve power only through a violent revolution. These may seem to be esoteric points, but they are the kind of seed-bed from which major ideological splits grow.

Later in the year the Soviet Union's image was badly damaged internationally, following its ruthless crushing of the Hungarian uprising. But in this case Mao was in absolute agreement with the Russians, and did not hesitate to condemn the developments in Hungary which had led to the uprising. Indeed, the Hungarian uprising caused Mao to make a major revision in his own thinking on the international order. In 1957 Zhou Enlai visited the Soviet Union and Eastern Europe, thus enhancing China's standing with the entire Soviet Bloc. In October of that year the Soviet Union and China concluded a secret military agreement, the details of which are still unclear. However, the Chinese said that Krushchev promised them a sample atom bomb and technical help to develop an independent nuclear capability. Whatever the truth of the matter, the Russians certainly gave the Chinese a great deal of technical assistance over the following months.

By now the cracks in the relationship were increasingly visible, and they coincided with a change of domestic policy in China. By then Mao had realised that the developmental blueprint which China had borrowed from the Soviet Union did not have all the answers, because China's economic base was agricultural rather than industrial. As explained in an earlier chapter, Mao had speeded up agricultural collectivisation at a pace and in a way of which the Russians did not approve. Mao had then launched the Hundred Flowers Movement, which filled the Russian leaders with consternation, and which they were relieved to see firmly suppressed. At the same time, to Krushchev's irritation, Mao was urging the Soviet Union to demonstrate international militancy.

In 1957 the Russians had launched two sputniks and an inter-continental ballistic missile. Mao was deeply impressed by these feats of technology, and felt that such a demonstration of socialist superiority should be used to put pressure on the United States. And it was at this time that Mao made his famous remark that 'The East wind has prevailed over the West wind.' But Krushchev realised that the balance of power was more than a matter of who had or had not launched a sputnik, and was in no mood to antagonise the United States. Furthermore, both the Russians and the Americans were appalled by what seemed an irresponsibly cavalier attitude on Mao's part towards the atom bomb. Having stated that it was likely that nuclear war could occur, Mao said that although 'half of mankind might die, the other half would remain, while imperialism would be razed to the ground and the whole world would become socialist'. He made a cool assessment of what would happen in China should its population be halved, and pointed to occasions in China's imperial past when this had happened. He said that despite these catastrophes China had always recovered. Mao did not appear to grasp that the aftermath of a nuclear war would be rather different from that of a war fought with bows and arrows.

1958 was a watershed year in the relations between the two countries. Mao launched the Great Leap Forward, and Krushchev deplored this attempt to skip one of the stages of socialism. Krushchev voiced these criticisms when he visited China in July, and his irritation was compounded when, shortly after he left, and without giving him any prior warning, Mao ordered a massive shelling of the offshore islands. These are a number of islands off the south-east China coast, opposite Fujian Province. The islands, of which Quemoy is the largest, are under the sovereignty of Taiwan, which is 125 miles away. At that time there were some 80 000 KMT troops and about 40 000 civilians on Quemoy, supplied by convoy from Taiwan. Although this was certainly not the first time that China had shelled the islands, on this occasion it also blockaded the Taiwan Straits, in the hope that the garrison at Quemoy would quickly surrender.

The immediate result was that the United States sent in its Seventh Fleet and its Fifth Air Force, and there was a general heightening of US military activity in the region. Instead of proving its might, it was China who backed down and stopped the bombardment. Later Mao said that he had no idea that lobbing a few shells at Quemoy would cause such a heightening of US activity in the area. It is always difficult to assess such statements. Certainly Mao had been incensed by the Americans' announcement in the previous year that they had deployed Matador missiles on Taiwan. These had a range of 650 miles, and therefore could have hit China. It was also possible that Mao launched the bombardment because he wanted to demonstrate China's strength in contrast with what he saw as growing Soviet pusillanimity. Although Krushchev sent a letter to President Eisenhower warning that any attack on China would be regarded as an attack on the Soviet Union, privately he deplored what he saw as a very rash act on Mao's part. By that time Krushchev was already seriously questioning his own wisdom in having agreed to help such an unpredictable ally to develop a nuclear capacity.

Earlier in 1958 Krushchev had written a letter to all world leaders, including Mao, to propose that nuclear testing be halted. Mao saw this as a ploy to stop the Chinese from developing their own nuclear capability. There were also arguments at the time over the possibility of sharing naval, air and communications facilities in China. Again, Mao saw this as a Soviet move to control China's armed forces.

But all these tensions in foreign relations were a direct reflection of an increasing radicalisation of domestic policy. China's analysts took the line that if the Soviet Union was adopting an 'unsocialist' foreign policy, then something must be rotten in the Soviet state. With the Great Leap Forward and its emphasis on 'red' rather than 'expert', Russian technicians lost their importance in China. Mao increasingly stressed the importance of self-reliance, and scorned 'worshipping things foreign', that is to say, the Soviet Union. Krushchev was beginning to see a change in the world order and was moving slowly towards better relations with the United States. He was irritated by Mao's determination to glory in revolution and international instability. In 1959 Soviet–US relations went a step further with Krushchev's visit to the United States' President's retreat at Camp David. Mao Zedong saw this not only as the ultimate betrayal, but also as a confirmation of his growing belief that China was the only country carrying the true socialist flag, and that it would have to carry it alone.

By the summer of 1959 there were clear indications that the Great Leap Forward was going badly wrong. As discussed in an earlier chapter, Mao had been ready to beat a retreat on his more radical policies, but he was subsequently so incensed by the attack of his then Minister of Defence, Peng Dehuai, on those same policies that it perversely stiffened his resolve to go full steam ahead. During that summer Krushchev not only criticised the Great Leap publicly for the first time but also abrogated the military treaty under which the Soviet Union was to help China develop a nuclear weapon. Mao was convinced that Peng was in collusion with Krushchev, and this further stiffened his resolve. In the following July the Soviet Union pulled out all its technicians and blueprints from China. Krushchev maintained that since the start of the Great Leap Forward they had not really had a role to play, so they might as well leave. This was a severe blow to China, as many heavy industrial projects were still in the developmental stage. This now confirmed Mao's belief that China would have to develop independently. The polemics against the Soviet Union grew very bitter, and it is often argued that the Chinese leadership was so obsessed by its deteriorating relations with the Soviet Union that it was unaware of the gathering domestic catastrophe.

The polemics were by no means one-sided. Krushchev accused Mao of being like Stalin, divorced from the reality of the changing international scene, vain and arrogant. In 1960 eighty-one Communist parties convened in Moscow and were witnesses to the unedifying spectacle of hours of bitter mutual attacks between the Soviet leaders on the one hand and Deng Xiaoping, representing the Chinese side, on the other. (It is worth bearing in mind the role Deng played at that time when considering the developments between China and the Soviet Union in the 1980s.) Only a handful of Communist parties supported the Chinese position, and 1960 marked an end to any sort of working relationship between the two countries whose relationship had at one time been described as 'close as lips and teeth'.

Everything seemed to come to a head at the same time. Not only was China heading for a domestic crisis and a break with its most important ally, but it was also facing confrontation with India. Although Peking and New Delhi had espoused the Five Principles of Peaceful Existence in 1954, they still had a dispute over the Sino-Indian border. The problem was the MacMahon line, drawn by the British in 1913–14, and recognised by the Indians but not by the Chinese. The line runs from Bhutan to Burma, and is supposed to follow the highest peaks south of the line in what India now calls the State of Arunachal Pradesh. Almost inevitably, no one can agree on the correct route which the line should have followed.

In 1958 it was revealed that the Chinese had built a new highway linking Xinjiang and Tibet across the Aksai Chin, which Indian maps showed belonged to India, along a completely different stretch of the border. Nehru complained to Zhou Enlai about the perceived encroachment by the Chinese, and Zhou replied that although the Chinese regarded the MacMahon line in the east as illegal, both sides should observe the actual line of control as it then stood. In other words, China would exchange Arunachal Pradesh, of little strategic interest, for the vital Aksai Chin, with its highway linking Xinjiang and Tibet. The Indians rejected the proposal, and there continued to be a number of incursions and counter-incursions. The situation was then greatly exacerbated by the revolt in Tibet in March 1959, when the Dalai Lama and some 100 000 followers fled to India, where they were granted asylum. Control of the passes leading from India into Tibet now became a matter of crucial importance to the Chinese. Not only were there militant Tibetans moving back and forth, but the Chinese also accused the Indians of allowing KMT and US agents to take advantage of the tension and operate out of India.

In August 1959 Chinese and Indian troops clashed in the eastern sector. The Chinese told the Soviet chargé d'affaires in New Delhi that the Indians were entirely to blame. However, the Soviet news agency, Tass, simply noted the clashes, with regret, but did not apportion blame. The Chinese regarded this as the first public airing of their dispute with the Soviet Union.

Before moving on to the Sino-Indian border war of 1962 this is an appropriate place to examine the vexed question of Tibet. The Chinese claim that for historical reasons Tibet is an integral part of China. This claim is not always easy to substantiate. For centuries Tibet was quite independent and the warrior kings of Tibet struck terror into the Chinese. The Chinese used the classic historical ways of striking alliances, including marrying a beautiful Chinese princess to one of the more troublesome Tibetan rulers.

The last imperial dynasty, the Qing (1644–1911) and the Republicans both claimed political control over Tibet and the north-western Province of Xinjiang, but in Tibet they failed to establish the necessary degree of dominance that might later have legitimised that control. In Tibet, Chinese control was challenged by the British at the beginning of this century, but an agreement between Britain and China signed in 1906 acknowledged Chinese sovereignty. Before the collapse of the imperial system in 1911, the eastern part of Tibet was under Peking's control, and in 1928 that sector was converted into the Provinces of Xikang (which no longer exists) and Qinghai. The central part of Tibet remained elusive until the Chinese took it by force in 1950. Reforms were instituted with a heavy hand, which eventually led to the 1959 revolt. This was crushed at great cost. The Tibetans put up a considerable fight and the Chinese found the warlike Khambas a force to be reckoned with, but they were no match for the vastly superior manpower and firepower of the Chinese troops.

Tibet always evokes great emotion, and it is difficult to be impartial about it. There is no doubt that the Chinese behaved like the worst of colonisers, imposing their language and customs, and for many years doing their utmost to erase Tibetan culture and religious beliefs. This cultural destruction reached its nadir during the Cultural Revolution, when thousands of monasteries were destroyed, sometimes by the marauding Red Guards, and sometimes by the monks and nuns themselves under the brutal supervision of the Red Guards. The Buddhist monks and nuns were disbanded and defrocked.

At the beginning of this decade China's top leaders started

to make inspection tours of Tibet, and were horrified by the prevailing situation. They found a poverty-stricken so-called Autonomous Region in which the people's rights had been trampled on by the mainly Han Chinese cadres. These same cadres loathed being in Tibet (for which they received substantial hardship pay), they despised the Tibetans, and the vast majority had never bothered to learn a word of the language. But such Han Chinese attitudes are not confined to those cadres working in Tibet. Time and time again foreigners visiting China have been incensed to hear a Han Chinese speak sneeringly about the 'minority' nationality peoples of China. The Han Chinese regard them as backward, lacking any sort of culture and generally a useless drain on the country. This is often very hard to believe when one hears the marvellous music and poetry of these people and watches their genuinely indigenous dances, as opposed to the ones which have been sinicised. It is also hard to accept such Han superiority when one looks around the Han areas of China, which are themselves often very poor and backward compared with many other countries.

There is no doubt that the minority peoples are a problem for the Chinese. There are some 80 million of them, and they live mainly in the sensitive border areas. Years of mutual antagonism have led to mistrust, and the Chinese sought to preclude any possible rebellion by colonising the border regions with large numbers of Han Chinese. This is particularly true of Inner Mongolia, Xinjiang and Tibet. Even so, this has not always stopped outbreaks of violence. There have been reports of clashes between the Chinese PLA and non-Han people in Xinjiang (which is largely Muslim), and the clashes in Tibet over the past eighteen months have been very well documented. Matters came to a head in March 1989 when there were demonstrations in Lhasa to mark the thirtieth anniversary of the Tibetan revolt. There was violence and bloodshed, and the Chinese authorities imposed martial law.

But one must also examine the situation from the Chinese point of view. They acknowledge that mistakes have been made in the treatment of the minority peoples, and are now making efforts to respect the culture and traditions of their minorities and to reinstate the use of their own languages, as in Tibet. The Chinese point to the fact that they have poured millions of dollars into developing these areas, especially Tibet. They cite the new roads and schools. However, the roads are to improve military access to the border, and for years the schools made every attempt to wipe out Tibetan culture. The Chinese maintain that before they took control of Tibet it was a poverty-stricken, feudal society, dominated by the monasteries and the landlords, where a man could be killed or mutilated for the slightest crime. They point to improved health care and child care, and although these still fall far short of other parts of China, they have improved.

There is a deep sense of frustration amongst the Han Chinese who feel that they have given so much, and are simply met by loathing and ingratitude. The problem is that the two cultures are poles apart. Religion is not just a part of life for the Tibetans, it *is* their life. They all yearn for the return of their spiritual leader, the Dalai Lama, but the Chinese will not permit him to live there permanently as they fear that his presence might lead to a popular uprising. The Dalai Lama has said that he will accept Chinese control of Tibet's military and foreign affairs if it is allowed genuine autonomy in other areas. That concession angered many of his followers, and was rejected by the Chinese. However, following the imposition of martial law, the Chinese authorities for the first time proposed direct talks with the Dalai Lama.

I doubt that there will ever be a wholly satisfactory solution to the problems of Tibet. There will always be tensions between its militant monks (now allowed to practise their calling once again) and the Chinese authorities, and the rulers and the ruled will never actually like each other. But it is highly unlikely that China will grant independence to Tibet, not even of the variety which it is offering to Hong Kong after 1997. The British, the Indians and the Russians have all, at various times, recognised the strategic importance of Tibet, and the Chinese regard it as vital to the security of their borders. However, following the Tiananmen Square massacre in June 1989, the rest of the world may have a heightened awareness of human rights problems throughout the whole of China, including Tibet.

Now back to China's relations with the outside world in the

early 1960s. During the Cuban crisis of 1962 the Chinese publicly issued a statement of support for Moscow, but privately accused it of adventurism for having put missiles into Cuba, and then of capitulationism for having removed them after US pressure. In August 1962 the Russians informed Peking that they had accepted an American proposal that those countries which had a nuclear capability should stop nuclear proliferation by banning the transfer of such knowledge to countries which did not yet have it. The Chinese regarded this as another ploy to prevent them from developing their own bomb, as indeed it was.

The same year also witnessed the short, but decisive, Sino-Indian border war. The Indians did what the Chinese had done in 1959, and started to probe across the MacMahon line into undisputed areas of Tibet on the eastern sector of the border. This prompted the Chinese PLA to sweep down on the Indian forces, and as they were in a much better strategic position they won a decisive victory. After a month the Chinese declared a unilateral cease-fire. Although the Chinese expelled the Indians from territory which they claimed as Chinese, they made no attempt to recover land which India had held before the dispute began but which China still claims – Arunachal Pradesh. The Russians reacted in exactly the same way as the Chinese had over Cuba. They issued a public statement of support, and then privately condemned them. Following the Sino-Indian clashes, India drew closer to the Soviet Union, which doubled its aid.

China may have been the victor in that external conflict, but internally the country was in economic chaos following the Great Leap Forward, and there were fears that Chiang Kai-shek would take advantage of the turmoil to launch an attack. There was also unrest in the north-west Province of Xinjiang, with thousands of non-Hans fleeing over the border into the Soviet Union. The Chinese believed, with some justification, that the Russians were fanning unrest.

As China settled in for a period of economic reconstruction, it continued to consolidate its foreign policy. There was an escalation of Sino-Soviet polemics following the signing of the partial Nuclear Test Ban Treaty by the Soviet Union with the United States and Britain in July 1963. Never one to pass up an opportunity for a colourful polemic, Mao now anathematised the Soviet Union as 'a Hitler type of dictatorship, they are a pack of ruffians, even worse than de Gaulle'. However, the two sides met to discuss their border problems in February 1964. The two countries share a border which is over 4000 miles long, and the Chinese maintain that large tracts of land were appropriated by imperial Russia under a series of what the Chinese call 'unequal treaties'. But despite their contention that the treaties were unequal the Chinese Communists said that they were willing to respect them and take them as a basis for negotiation. Then on 14 October Nikita Krushchev fell from power, and on 16 October China exploded its first atom bomb, becoming the first developing nation to join the nuclear club.

During 1963 and 1964 many countries in the 'intermediate zone' recognised China. But probably a far greater prize for the Chinese was recognition by the French, despite the attack on de Gaulle only a few months previously. During the winter of 1963–64 Zhou Enlai visited ten African countries , and there was a strengthening of Sino–Pakistani relations. In many ways 1964 was a watershed year. The Chinese had no major confrontations, and they continued to build their international relations. By the end of the year fifty countries recognised China rather than Chiang Kai-shek's government in Taiwan, although the latter still held the 'China' seat in the United Nations. But now the forthcoming Vietnam war was casting its shadow, and Peking increased its support for Hanoi's position. However, when war broke out in 1965, the Chinese decided not to enter the war directly, so risking open confrontation with the Americans, but to limit their help to advisers and war material.

The Chinese suffered a setback in 1965 when they proposed that the Afro-Asian nations should form a rival organisation to the United Nations. This proposal stemmed from President Sukarno of Indonesia's removal of his country from the UN, which Mao had always condemned as a mere tool of the United States and the Soviet Union. However, many of the Afro-Asian states were becoming irritated by China's aggressively articulated view that only China had the correct answers to the international situation. Even the smooth Zhou Enlai managed to raise eyebrows during his African tour when he announced that 'revolutionary prospects are excellent throughout the African continent'. The leaders of the countries which he was visiting thought that they had already brought about their revolutions and cast out the colonial oppressors, so no other revolutions were necessary. China's reputation was further compromised in an abortive coup attempt by the Communists in Indonesia. The Indonesian General Suharto, who used the insurrection as a pretext to snatch power, blamed China for allegedly supporting the Indonesian Communists. In 1967 he froze relations with China, and only in 1989 did he begin normalisation talks. This confirmed the fears of the South-East Asian nations that China was a dangerous ally, and a fomentor of revolution.

By February 1966 the Afro-Asian Solidarity Organisation, exasperated by China's attempts to split them from the UN and the Soviet Union, reacted by expelling Chinese delegates from a meeting in Nicosia, and five countries broke off relations with Peking. Then, as the Cultural Revolution gathered pace, with its attendant xenophobia, even erstwhile allies were not safe. Whilst the Chinese press constantly stressed that the *people* of the various countries under attack 'warmly love Chairman Mao' and the Chinese people and government had no quarrel with *them*, it was the governments of those countries which were beyond the pale. Embassies representing countries with varying political systems, from France to Indonesia, India to Czechoslovakia were the victims of mass demonstrations, and their diplomats were frequently subjected to very rough treatment. Overseas Chinese were whipped up by local 'Red Guards' to hold demonstrations against the countries in which they were resident. In London the Chinese Embassy in Portland Place became a lively battleground, with Chinese diplomats wielding axes and staves.

Not surprisingly, the Soviet Embassy was accorded the same kind of treatment as the British Mission. Although the Red Guards stopped short of burning it down they kept it under siege for two weeks. By the end of 1967 the Chinese had managed to pick a fight with twenty-five countries, and everyone was wondering whether sanity would ever be restored in the country. The countries of South-East Asia, increasingly suspicious of the revolutionary stridency of China, had had all their worst fears confirmed by China's support of their insurgent Communist parties. China's support for the North Vietnamese government in its battle against the United States fuelled their fears that Communism was percolating through the region.

The Chinese leadership, and that included Mao Zedong as well as the more pragmatic elements (very few of whom were still in power) like Zhou Enlai, realised that international alienation had gone far enough. A major exercise started in fence-mending, and an awareness of the dangers of diplomatic isolation was reinforced by a series of very sharp clashes along the Sino-Soviet border in 1969. The Soviet-inspired Warsaw Pact invasion of Czechoslovakia the year before had been roundly condemned by the Chinese, and seen as a portent that the Russians were capable of mounting a similar attack against China. The Chinese claimed that the Russians had made several incursions across their border in 1968, and then at the beginning of March 1969 the PLA shot thirty-four Russian soldiers on a disputed island, Zhenbao, in the Ussuri River, which marks part of the north-eastern border between the two countries.

At that time the Russians still maintained that the border ran along the south side of the river, which would have made all the islands Soviet territory. The Chinese claimed that the border ran along the Thalweg, or deepest channel of the river, and that the islands on the south side of the Thalweg belonged to them. The Chinese certainly had right on their side according to the usual practice of international law. After the Zhenbao incident there were colossal demonstrations in China against this latest act of 'Soviet aggression'. Two weeks later the Chinese attacked again, but this time the Russians were much better prepared and they killed some 800 Chinese soldiers.

Fanning a domestic fear of war with their northern neighbour may have been a good way of distracting the attention of the Chinese people from the chaos at home, but since both China and the Soviet Union had a nuclear device, it was an appallingly dangerous game. The Chinese realised that they had no real allies and very few friends, and it was at this lowest point that the unthinkable happened – China began to mend fences with the United States. It was not that Mao believed that the United States had in any way changed from being a capitalist, imperialist power, but he was once again going to use his old tactic of using a lesser evil to combat a greater one. Furthermore, it was clear that the United States was fighting a losing battle against the North Vietnamese, and that this would diminish its influence in Asia.

By December 1970 Mao had told the American journalist Edgar Snow that he would be happy to meet United States' President Richard Nixon. As Nixon, within days of taking office, had asked Secretary of State Henry Kissinger to see what could be done to improve Sino–US relations, he was ready to accept the Chinese advances. The world woke up to the impending thaw when an American ping-pong team visited China in April 1971. Kissinger paid a preparatory visit to China in July that year, and then the arch-Republican met the arch-Communist on 21 February 1972.

The decision to sink its differences with the United States so swiftly was a source of great contention in China, and we know that many of the leftist leaders were against it. When the Zhou–Nixon Communiqué, otherwise known as the Shanghai Communiqué, was signed in 1972 there were murmurings that it contained no American guarantees that they would cease to arm the KMT on Taiwan, and this was to rise up and haunt Deng Xiaoping later on.

After Deng returned to power in 1973, and before he was disgraced again in 1976, he decided that China needed foreign technology if it were ever to improve its economy. The Gang of Four were to accuse him of having imported far too much foreign plant, although that is hard to quantify. However, China's foreign trade certainly did shoot up from US $3.9 billion in 1969 to US $14 billion in 1975, and China for the first time incurred a large trade deficit and had to borrow abroad to pay for it. In a rush of national pride and a desire to have nothing but the best, during the mid-1970s China certainly imported equipment that was often far too sophisticated for its needs, and which then lay gathering dust, as no one knew how to use or repair it.

After Mao's death and Deng's return to power in 1977 there was one question which was to exercise the Chinese leadership time and time again: how far should China compromise its independence by importing more than it could afford, and how far should it let itself be beholden to the country supplying the plant and technology? The Chinese had learnt a very bitter lesson from their symbiotic relationship with the

Soviet Union and were determined never again to rely wholly on one country.

That was easier said than done. China's relations with Japan improved to the extent that the two countries signed a Treaty of Friendship in 1978, and the Japanese established an almost unassailable position as China's largest trading partner, after the entrepôt mecca of Hong Kong. Given the readiness of Japan to assume this position, the geographical propinquity and the cultural affinity between the two nations, this was a natural development. But the relationship has not been without its serious problems. The Chinese soon ran up a huge trade deficit with the Japanese. As the economic reforms in China brought greater prosperity, and as Chinese firms had greater autonomy, there seemed to be an insatiable desire for Japanese goods, including cars and electronic manufactures. This reached alarming levels by the mid-1980s, and then there was a backlash. Not only was the Chinese government worried about a wildly overheating economy in 1985, but Chinese students were beginning to demonstrate against 'Japanese economic imperialism'. There was a conscious decision drastically to reduce imports of Japanese goods, and the results were almost immediately apparent in a sharply reduced trade deficit.

The relationship with Japan is deeply ambivalent, and given the recent conflicts between the two countries this is hardly surprising. Not only was China humiliated by the Japanese occupation of Manchuria, but the Sino-Japanese war happened within the lifetime of many millions of Chinese who are still alive today. The Chinese estimate that 10 million of them were killed in that war, many under conditions of appalling brutality. The Japanese subjected Chinese in camps in the north-east to medical experimentation, including exposure to bacilli, vivisection and similar experiments to those used on Japanese prisoners of war elsewhere in Asia. Even as relations with Japan were improving, the Chinese built a museum in the city of Harbin in North-East China to commemorate the horrors of the Sino-Japanese war.

Tensions between the two countries are constantly rising to the surface. China's economic dependence on Japan is a major irritant. At root is the memory of the 1930s and 1940s and the feeling that, in a less brutal way, Japan still clings to the imperialist vision of a Greater Asian Co-prosperity Sphere. Japan is the workshop and sells its manufactures; the rest of the world buys them and supplies the raw materials. This economic tension heightens political irritants. When the former Japanese Prime Minister Yasuhiro Nakasone, visited the Yasukuni Shrine – the shrine to Japan's war dead – the Chinese complained about this insult to the memories of those Chinese killed by the Japanese.

The Chinese also complain about the rewriting of Japanese school textbooks by the Japanese Ministry of Education. In 1986 a textbook was amended to tone down the role played by the Japanese during the Sino-Japanese war, and it was more or less explicitly stated that if the Chinese had not resisted so stoutly in Nanjing it would not have been necessary to massacre them. Then in April 1988 a cabinet minister denied that Japan had been the aggressor in the Second World War, and said that it was merely defending itself against colonisation by the white races. The Chinese were outraged, and the minister was sacked. When the Japanese Foreign Minister visited shortly afterwards, followed by the then Prime Minister Noboru Takeshita in August, both went bearing gifts of very substantial soft loan packages as emollients. (Since then Mr Takeshita has been forced to apologise for ambiguous remarks which he himself made about the origins of the war.) The Chinese have always expected to be given very favourable trade and loan terms by the Japanese because, as they frequently point out, they were the only country not to claim reparations from the Japanese after the war. They complain that since 1972 Japan has only provided 8.7 per cent of China's cumulative investment.

Japan's response to the crushing of the demonstrations in Peking in June 1989 was somewhat muted and confused. Initially Japan 'deplored' the event, but subsequently the Prime Minister said that the actions of the Chinese army had been 'unforgivable', and announced a virtual freeze on aid. However, after the initial shock had worn off, a large number of Japanese businessmen returned to China, prompting a rebuke by the Japanese Foreign Minister. And indeed, a large number of Japanese companies had not closed their offices in the first place.

It is too soon to say, with Japan as with all of China's other trading partners, what will happen in the field of trade and investment in the coming months. Many private businessmen will be worried about future political instability. Despite assurances from Deng Xiaoping that the 'open door' and pragmatic economic policies will continue as before, there is no guarantee at this stage that this will be so. And there will also be some companies which will hesitate to invest in a country whose government has incurred international opprobrium.

However, as the swift return by many Japanese businessmen showed, Japan's trading relationship is a special one. Japan will probably always be one of China's top three trading partners. Until the Tiananmen Massacre the Japanese government had been trying to persuade Japanese businessmen to invest more in China. Taiwan and South Korea are now becoming more and more expensive as manufacturing bases, and, perhaps more importantly, were becoming serious competitors to Japan as exporters and investors in China itself, following dramatic foreign policy shifts in Taipei and Seoul. So, despite the considerable problems of trading with China, the Japanese have generally thought it worth the trouble.

The problems of trading with China are not exclusive to Japanese companies. Before the burgeoning of trade following the economic reforms, the difficulties tended to centre on lack of hard currency and the slowness of a centralised bureaucracy. Subsequently, with power devolved to the provinces, the foreign businessman often found himself being passed from bureau to bureau, never knowing who had the ultimate authority to decide anything. Having signed a contract, he often discovered that the organisation with which he signed it had been disbanded, and the contract was therefore declared invalid. Or the individual who signed it had changed jobs, and his successor would not honour the contract. The old saying that a Chinese man's word is his bond has long since become a myth, and the business world is full of cautionary tales of broken contracts. If a commodity price changed, the Chinese had no hesitation in breaking the contract and demanding a better price. One was beginning to hear tales of people who had been trading with China for decades suing the Chinese for breach of contract. Although the Chinese would prefer to buy technology, the fear that they will then breach copyright has held back many foreign firms and was a further cause of friction. Costs of labour, office space and services all soared in China and again, this meant that smaller firms simply could not afford to venture into the field. A gradual disillusionment with China was already driving many firms away.

China has moved far in its relations with its Asian neighbours over the past decade. There were great tensions in the region in 1978. In December that year the Vietnamese invaded Cambodia, which for three years had been under the murderous heel of Pol Pot and the Khmer Rouge. Pol Pot was a friend to China. Some of his fanatical egalitarianism he owed to Mao. But more crucially he turned Cambodia into an anti-Vietnamese bastion. China was enraged with Vietnam – for turning to the Soviet Union, for mistreating its ethnic Chinese population, for claiming remote islands which China claims are its territory and, more generally, for failing to 'pay tribute' to the regional overlord in Peking. They saw Vietnam as a Soviet stooge – its 'Cuba in Asia' – seeking to colonise Laos and Cambodia. Although Deng Xiaoping had been keen to launch an attack on the Vietnamese as soon as they entered Cambodia in the early winter, he waited until relations with the United States had been normalised. The signing ceremony took place on 16 December 1978, and the Chinese then felt that with such an ally the Russians would not open a second front against them on their northern border if they were to attack Vietnam. And they were right. The Chinese launched an attack on the Vietnamese 'to teach them a lesson' in February 1979, withdrawing their troops again in March, having been trounced by the Vietnamese.

Apart from their brief brush with India in 1962, the Chinese had not fought a war since Korea in the early 1950s, whereas the Vietnamese had been in an almost permanent state of war. Not only were the Chinese fighting battle-hardened veterans, but veterans equipped with very sophisticated weaponry supplied by the Soviet Union. And they knew the territory on which they were fighting much better than the Chinese. It is said that the Chinese were using maps drawn up in the Qing Dynasty. The story may be apocryphal, but it gives one an idea of the disparity between the two sides.

In March 1979 I was in China accompanying a small group

of 'eminent persons', as the Chinese call them, and we had a meeting with Deng Xiaoping. It was immediately after the confrontation, and Deng said to us that it had been a military disaster but a political victory, and that China would do it again if necessary. Yet China did not attempt such action again in the following years. By a political victory one presumes that Deng meant that China had demonstrated that it was ready to fight on behalf of its allies, and to help to secure the isolation and impoverishment of Vietnam. China wanted to 'bleed white' its erstwhile comrade-in-arms. However, the negative result was that China's most important allies were dismayed by the Chinese action, and the South-East Asian nations saw it as a sign of growing Chinese hegemony in the region. Once again they could see shadows of the past, when China openly supported South-East Asian Communist movements, and here it was now trying to shore up the most abominable of them all – the Khmer Rouge.

In September 1979 the Chinese initiated talks with the Soviet Union in an attempt to improve relations between the two countries, but the Soviet invasion of Afghanistan brought them to an abrupt halt. The Chinese roundly condemned the Soviet action and drew closer both to Pakistan on the regional plane and to the United States at superpower level. As the Soviet Union became more isolated internationally because of Afghanistan and its support for the Vietnamese occupation of Cambodia, so China steadily improved its international image. In 1979 the then Prime Minister and Party Chairman, Hua Guofeng, visited France, West Germany, Britain and Italy. In 1980, for the first time, China reversed its position on the inevitability of war and said that, if the expansion of the 'hegemonists' could be curbed, war was preventable.

The advent of the Reagan administration in the United States in 1980 brought new tensions to the relationship, as it was far more vigorously anti-Communist than the Carter administration under which they had established diplomatic relations. The Americans took a tougher line on Taiwan, stepping up arms sales. However, this led to a hardening of Deng Xiaoping's attitude, and in 1982 the two sides signed another communiqué in which the Americans agreed not to increase arms sales to Taiwan beyond the level of the preceding year, and eventually to reduce them 'to a final resolution'.

As with Sino-Japanese relations, so Sino-US relations have been of enormous importance to China, but even before the events of June 1989 they were not without their tensions. The Chinese felt that the Americans should relax still further their restrictions on the export of advanced technology to China and they complained that the Americans only imported 1 per cent of their total commodity imports from China. China also grumbled that although it had overtaken Taiwan as the United States' main textile supplier, American investment in China has been only a minute fraction of its total overseas aid.

A constant source of friction between the two countries was the question of human rights in China, and the behaviour of the Chinese towards the Tibetans. Even before the suppression of the pro-democracy demonstrations exacerbated that aspect of Sino-US tension, questions were frequently asked in Congress, and motions put forward to censure the Chinese. American Right to Life groups have been vociferous in their condemnation of forced abortion in China.

Following the forcible suppression of the mass demonstrations in Peking in early June this year, the tensions between the two countries have heightened. The United States criticised the actions of the Chinese army, and the Chinese authorities reacted sharply by rejecting the United States' (and other countries') 'interference in China's internal affairs'. The United States and Britain suspended sales of military equipment and cancelled projected military co-operation. The situation was exacerbated by the fact that the dissident scientist, Fang Lizhi and his wife sought refuge in the US Embassy in Peking. The Peking authorities promptly issued a warrant for their arrest, accusing them of inciting the student unrest and of counter-revolutionary activities.

Provided that the Chinese are not seen to carry out executions on a large scale in the months ahead, relations with the United States, as with many other countries, will probably slowly return to a greater degree of normality. Most countries recognise the dangers of completely ostracising China, as this could engender isolationism and xenophobia. However, in the United States there is a large Chinese community, and many thousands of Chinese students will continue to monitor events in China. American public opinion, previously very well-disposed towards China, was appalled by the actions of the Chinese army, and has been loud in its condemnation. Many politicians, both Republicans and Democrats, have called for sanctions. In the face of such public anger, it will be difficult for the US government to ignore reports of widespread suppression. Sadly, however, there are many brutal and repressive governments around the world and the governments and businessmen of democratic countries have continued to have normal political and business relations with them.

Until June 1989 there was a great improvement in relations with countries which for many years had been distinctly strained. In the Soviet Union the rise to power of Mikhail Gorbachev paved the way not only for a great improvement in Sino-Soviet relations, but also led to much better relations with the entire Eastern Bloc with which China had had very little contact since the Sino-Soviet split. The only exception to that rule was Romania, which had long enjoyed China's approval because of its independent foreign policy. In June 1987 Zhao Ziyang, then Prime Minister and Acting Party Secretary, visited East Germany, Czechoslovakia, Poland, Hungary and Bulgaria. 1988 saw a series of return visits by both heads of state and Party chiefs from countries in the Eastern Bloc, and China has now restored party-to-party ties with all the countries of the Soviet Bloc including, most recently, the Soviet Union. But apart from East Germany, which supported the Chinese government's suppression of the demonstrations, and Romania, which made no comment, other countries in the Eastern Bloc deplored the action.

With the outbreak of peace around the world over the past two years, there was also an improvement in relations with some of China's long-time enemies. Formal relations between China and India were resumed in 1981 and, after a series of talks on their border dispute, India finally conceded in 1988 that a settlement of the border issue could wait, and normal relations develop alongside. Minor clashes in 1986 and 1987 reinforced this view. The Chinese still claim 38 000 square miles of Indian territory – Arunachal Pradesh, which the Indians declared a state in 1986, to the annoyance of the Chinese. And the Indians claim some 14 500 square miles in Aksai Chin, where China built its highway in the 1950s.

When Prime Minister Rajiv Gandhi visited China in December 1988 no progress was made on the border dispute, but Rajiv agreed to set the issue on one side and it was concluded that a joint working group should be set up at Vice-ministerial level to address the border question. Both sides agreed that they need to increase their trade, which in 1988 was only US $185 million. But China is wary of India's increasing nuclear capacity, and its more visible military role in the region, as in Sri Lanka and, most recently, in the Maldives.

Without a doubt the most significant foreign policy change for the entire region in the 1980s is the burgeoning relationship between China and the Soviet Union. The first approaches were made under Leonid Brezhnev's leadership, with the start of a dreary series of six-monthly 'normalisation talks' in 1982, but the pace quickened considerably after the iconoclastic Mr Gorbachev became Secretary General of the Soviet Communist Party in 1985. Gorbachev was only too aware that if his efforts were to be concentrated on economic reforms at home, he would have to decrease military tension abroad. The Soviet presence in Afghanistan was bleeding the Soviet economy, as was the US $3 million a day which the Russians were pouring into Vietnam. The various conflicts in Africa supported by the Soviet Union were also a financial drain, and the costs of keeping up vast numbers of men and *matériel* on the NATO flank were colossal.

One area where Gorbachev could see a possibility for military economy was on the border with China, where the Russians had fifty-one divisions. The Chinese had consistently said that there were three prerequisites to normalising their relations with the Soviet Union. These were: troop reductions on their common border; the withdrawal of Soviet troops from Afghanistan; and the cessation of support for the Vietnamese occupation of Cambodia.

On 28 July 1986 Mr Gorbachev made his famous speech in Vladivostock. His proposals for decreasing tension in the Far East were largely ignored by the world's press, so interested were they in the parts of the speech that applied to Europe. One major concession which he made to the Chinese was to agree to the Chinese demand that their common border should run along the main channel of the Amur and Ussuri Rivers – the Thalweg principle. He also made a commitment to reduce the number of troops in Afghanistan and along the Sino-Mongolian border. Just as Mikhail Gorbachev always manages to catch the West by surprise by the boldness of his proposals, he was equally successful with the Chinese. It took them a month to consider their response, and then it was lukewarm. They responded much more enthusiastically to Mr Gorbachev's Krasnoyarsk speech in September 1988, which was largely a confirmation of his earlier speech. But by then the international situation had changed, and the Chinese knew that they were in danger of being left out if they continued to be aloof.

Mr Gorbachev fulfilled his promises. There are now only about one million Russian troops on the Sino-Soviet and Sino-Mongolian border, where previously there were over two, and these will be reduced still further. Soon the number of Soviet troops in Mongolia will be fewer than 15 000 and with the gradual pull-out of troops from Mongolia, Sino-Mongolian relations have also improved. There has been a reduction of Soviet forces in the Soviet Far East, although it is possible that those left behind are better equipped. When the Soviets took the United States by surprise and agreed to the 'Double Zero' option, it led to the signing of the INF Treaty to eliminate land-based intermediate-range missiles from Asia as well as Europe. So the Soviet Union's 160 SS20s in the Far East were removed without China having to make any concessions in return. And then the Russians kept their word about the troop pull-out from Afghanistan.

As the other two obstacles disappeared, the Chinese placed increased importance on the third – Cambodia. But they realised that they were losing the propaganda war against the Soviet Union, and were open to accusations of not wanting peace in the region. And although the Chinese were restrainedly positive in their welcome for the INF Agreement, Deng Xiaoping was aware that the great international decisions were being made without him.

There are at least four main reasons why Deng delayed for so long in relenting towards the Gorbachev overtures. One is the traditional Chinese belief that everyone should come to them, in the style of the old suzerain states of imperial times. And everyone did. Even the most dyed-in-the-wool anti-Communists beat a path to the Chinese door, and the former arch-revisionists were not going to be allowed to do less. An equally strong reason is that Deng himself was one of the most fierce polemicists in the battle of words with the Soviets in the 1960s, and until recently those visceral feelings may have been even stronger than political expediency. But then Deng and Gorbachev came to need each other. Both had embarked on radical and potentially dangerous paths towards reform, and had lessons to learn from each other. Thirdly, the Chinese know how to bargain. By playing hard-to-get they won most of the concessions from Moscow. And finally, Deng felt that he could not afford to alienate the United States by enveloping himself with unbecoming ardour in Mr Gorbachev's bear hug.

For several years there had been a steady exchange of cultural and scientific delegations. There had also been extensive student exchanges, and the Soviet Union is co-operating with China to upgrade the industrial plant which the Russians helped to build in the 1950s. There is lively cross-border trade, and now even tourists cross daily at the border in Heilongjiang. Total trade in 1988 was about US $3.2 billion, and is rising fast. In February 1987 talks resumed to settle the border question, and in November 1988 agreement was reached on a long stretch of the eastern sector.

In December 1988, the Chinese Foreign Minister, Qian Qichen (a Soviet specialist) visited the Soviet Union, the first such visit for over thirty years. The Soviet Foreign Minister, Eduard Shevardnadze returned the visit in early February 1989. During that visit it was agreed that a Sino-Soviet summit would take place in Peking in May 1989, the first for three decades. Although the Russians have made most of the concessions in the relationship, the Chinese have recently, and without much fanfare, changed their position on Cambodia. Initially they said that they would not hold a summit until all Vietnamese troops were out of Cambodia. Some 50 000 are still there, but should be out by September 1989. But the Chinese accepted that the Russians were pushing the Vietnamese to withdraw. The Chinese have also accepted that there will have to be an international peace-keeping force in Cambodia. They know that the tripartite coalition of Prince Sihanouk, Son Sann and the Khmer Rouge has always been an uneasy one, and will be even more so when the Vietnamese-backed Hun Sen's government in Pnomh Penh becomes part of the equation. They accept that the Khmer Rouge must not be allowed to return to power (and as they are generally believed to be the most effective fighting force, thanks to Chinese military aid, it is possible that they will) and that Prince Sihanouk must head the quadripartite government. A less well-publicised reason why the Chinese may have accepted the need for an international peace-keeping force is a fear that, in the final analysis, it might not be the Khmer Rouge who would emerge victorious from a civil war, but Hun Sen's troops.

The first Sino-Soviet summit for thirty years took place in Peking from 15–18 May, amidst demonstrations by hundreds of thousands of students and residents of Peking. Although it had been assumed that the Chinese authorities would have acted either to crush or to defuse the demonstrations, which by then had been going on for nearly a month before the Soviet leader arrived, they had not done so.

President Gorbachev's visit was severely disrupted. The welcoming ceremony had to be shifted from Tiananmen Square, then occupied by the demonstrators, to the airport. In order to attend meetings with Chinese leaders, the Russians were unceremoniously smuggled into the Great Hall of the People through side doors, and much of Mr Gorbachev's programme had to be abandoned as the centre of Peking was at a standstill. Mr Gorbachev was carefully non-committal when asked for his views on the demonstrations.

But the political crisis in China distracted the world's attention from the truly extraordinary nature of the summit. Characteristically, Mikhail Gorbachev made proposals which took everyone by surprise by their range and imagination. After thirty years of coldness which occasionally erupted into hostilities, he proposed the effective demilitarisation of the 4500-mile-long border between the two countries. He suggested that there should be a massive withdrawal of troops, and that those which remained should occupy an exclusively defensive position. He also announced that on the very day of his arrival in Peking, three full-strength divisions of troops would be withdrawn from Mongolia, leaving only some 10 000–15 000.

As a sign of his wish to help bring peace to the Asian region he also announced that sixteen battleships were to be removed from the Soviet Pacific Fleet, and that the 200 000 troop cut in Soviet Asia, to be completed by 1990, would include the withdrawal of 120 000 troops which directly threatened China. In all, eleven air force regiments were also to be disbanded in the region, and the Soviet ground forces reduced by eleven divisions.

Both sides urged an increase in trade, which is still proportionally very small. And with party-to-party relations now restored, both countries will be sending delegates to each other's party conferences for the first time since the early 1960s. There will also be a resumption of contacts between the respective Party Central Committees. But although the final communiqué indicated increased common ground between the two countries (the first time for decades that the Chinese had acknowledged having *anything* in common with the USSR), it was clear that there were areas where the Chinese had resisted Soviet persuasion. President Gorbachev was keen to have joint military co-operation, but the Chinese feared that that might jeopardise their military ties with the USA (ironic in the light of recent developments). The Rus sians were also eager to have a joint statement calling for the withdrawal of United States' troops from South Korea. Again, the Chinese did not agree.

The events in Tiananmen Square and the international reaction have posed something of a dilemma for the Soviet leader. Although the Soviet Union finally criticised what had happened, it was in somewhat muted tones. A strong condemnation would not only have angered the Chinese leadership, but might also have angered Mr Gorbachev's hardline critics. After all, would the Soviet leader want mass pro-democracy demonstrations going on for weeks in the centre of Moscow? But the confident assertion by the Chinese that if the West cuts off trade and aid then they will simply turn to the Soviet Union is easier said than done. Moscow cannot provide China with the advanced technology which it needs for its economic development, and China does not want roubles in exchange for its exports. It wants dollars. Furthermore, the Soviet Union has increasing links with many countries in the Pacific region, and would probably be unwilling to allow its relationship with an unpopular Chinese government to damage those nascent links.

And whilst we are looking at changing alliances, South Korea is a interesting example. It is not that China has abandoned its old ally, North Korea, but both China and the Soviet Union have become impatient with the time-warped view of the Kim Il-Sung regime. Its well-documented acts of terrorism are an embarrassment to its allies, and it is also a financial embarrassment, as it plays Moscow off against Peking to secure charity hand-outs. North Korea was dealt a severe blow when China and the Soviet Union attended the Seoul Games in 1988. Both continue to supply North Korea with military equipment, but the last thing that they want is confrontation on the peninsula, and they strongly support moves towards peace talks. In South Korea itself there is now a government much less hostile towards Communism, and eager to trade with the Communist countries. Although China has resisted South Korean moves towards establishing diplomatic relations (China cannot be seen to be operating a 'Two Koreas' policy) there has been a dramatic increase in both indirect and direct trade. Trade in 1988 was estimated to be at least US $2 billion, and this was cemented by a formal trade agreement in September 1988.

And what of those 'problems left over from history', as the Chinese call them? The Portuguese colony of Macao will be returned to China in 1999 and it will be interesting to see whether the Chinese will feel obliged to clean up the extremely lucrative gambling and gold smuggling, or whether they will turn a blind eye and continue to reap enormous financial benefits.

Hong Kong was always more of a problem, and following the events of June this year, it is now an even greater one. According to the Anglo-Chinese Agreement of 1984 it will be returned to China in 1997. The Chinese agreed to a 'One country, two systems' framework. Under this, the Chinese government agreed that Hong Kong would be allowed to continue on capitalist lines for at least fifty years, and probably much longer. But Chinese troops are eventually to be stationed there, and a new set of laws to meet the new situation is being drafted by Peking. Even before June there was agitation in Hong Kong over how the Chief Executive was to be appointed after 1997, and the degree of democracy which would prevail in the colony by the time it was handed back to China.

Large numbers of Chinese were not prepared to gamble on the answers, and were insuring against future problems by acquiring an additional nationality. Favoured passports are American, Australian and Canadian. Many Hong Kong people have felt betrayed by Britain, and maintained from the outset that those who wished to emigrate to Britain should have been allowed to do so. They can now point to the decision of the Portuguese government to allow some 100 000 people of Chinese descent who were born in Macao to take full Portuguese nationality. This will allow them to settle in Portugal or, eventually, any country in the EEC. However, some 3.25 million were born in Hong Kong and could credibly claim to be British. Apprehension about such a large number of potential immigrants to Britain was certainly the major factor in the decision by the British government not to grant full British nationality, with its attendant right of abode, to those Chinese born in Hong Kong.

However, the Chinese government's iron-fisted response to the pro-democracy demonstrations in Peking has swiftly sharpened the political awareness of the people of Hong Kong, and raised international concern about their future. Unprecedented demonstrations of anything up to half a million people took place in Hong Kong to protest at the killings in Peking. A fear that at some time in the future the Chinese government might use equally repressive methods against protesters in Hong Kong aroused people from all walks of life to voice their fears. There was a considerable increase in the queues outside foreign consulates as people applied for visas.

Understandably, in the light of what happened in Peking, there were calls from politicians and ordinary members of the public both in Britain and Hong Kong to do something to assure the people of Hong Kong that they would not be abandoned should things look bad for Hong Kong. Solutions put forward included the right of abode for all who could claim British nationality. Other proposals included the drawing up of an international agreement under which various countries around the world would grant a safe haven to the people of Hong Kong *after* 1997, should the situation demand it. Realistically, it is too soon after the event to do anything dramatic about Hong Kong, although every possible course must be examined. By 1997 a very different sort of government may be in power in China, and whilst I have never believed that China's socialism would coexist happily with Hong Kong's laissez faire capitalism, by then many new factors may have entered the equation.

One main reason why the Chinese government agreed to the 'One country, two systems' framework for Hong Kong was to send out reassuring signals to Taiwan, which they want to entice back into the embrace of the motherland. Even before the Tiananmen Massacre in June the Taiwanese government had been hostile to the mainland. Although the gradual disappearance of the old guard in Taiwan has led to a considerable improvement in relations, the KMT government still maintains, rather improbably, that it is the legitimate government of China.

Following the death of Chiang Kai-shek in 1975 his son, Chiang Ching-kuo, permitted a slight breach in the wall of hostility, and following *his* death in January 1988 his successor, the Taiwan-born Lee Teng-hui, allowed a sharp acceleration of the pace. From November 1987 Taiwanese were allowed to visit relatives on the mainland, and during 1988 at least 300 000 did so. Mainlanders are also permitted to visit ailing relatives or attend their funerals. In 1988 indirect trade was over US $2.6 billion, and there are at least 200 joint ventures between the two countries. The east-coast port of Ningbo is constructing a dock for the exclusive use of Taiwanese ships. An indication of the improvement in relations is that both sides agreed that they would no longer pay huge rewards to defecting air force pilots, events which previously were turned into huge propaganda circuses.

It is far too soon to say to what extent China's relations with Taiwan will be affected in the light of the events in Tiananman Square in June this year. Some businessmen may be reluctant to invest in China, and the number of Taiwanese visitors to China will certainly diminish. Indeed, China's tourist industry in general has already been very badly hit. At present Taiwan agrees that it is a part of China, and as long as that continues, I do not believe that China will try to take it by force. Not only would it be a mutually destructive encounter, but it would cause immense damage to China's relations with the United States and with other countries in the region.

Only if Taiwan were to declare itself independent might

China feel forced into action, and that could possibly take the form of a blockade (Taiwan has few raw materials, and a blockade could be very effective), but that would cause tension with a number of countries which trade with Taiwan, and would make China look like a superpower bully. However, more and more young Tiawanese are calling for independence, and the events of June may reinforce that impetus. Already we have been seeing a transition from a mainland-born elite who came over with Chiang Kai-shek, to a younger generation, with ancestral roots on the island going back centuries. They regard the 'One China' pipe-dream as nostalgic nonsense, and now will be even less attracted to that concept. How China would react to a popular demand for independence will depend very much on the kind of government which is ruling in Peking at the time, but no Chinese government, whether hardline or relatively liberal, would regard the prospect with equanimity.

As with relations between China and Taiwan, it is too soon to say what will happen in the short term in China's international relations. At present there is a huge sense of moral outrage in very many countries, and in the immediate future China will probably lose its position as the country to which every other country was beating a path. But if the situation calms, and there is a diminution of repression, then *Realpolitik* may once again prevail. A China in isolation would not be beneficial either to the Asian region, nor in terms of international relations. One must remember that this year alone there were summit meetings between China and the United States, China and the USSR and Prime Ministerial level meetings between China and Japan. China has now become too important a participant in world affairs to be able to retreat into itself. It has a large foreign debt to service, without having the foreign currency reserves with which to do it, so it will need foreign trade and investment, however much it may dislike the idea of simultaneously importing Western ideas.

However, one hopes that governments and businessmen will not be too ready to forget the events of June. Although China cannot and should not be ignored, any more than any other nation, the other members of the United Nations should continue to make known their extreme disapproval of what happened in Peking. It must be made clear that if China wishes to be a fully-fledged member of the international community, with all the benefits which that entails, then it also bears the onus to behave according to internationally accepted norms of conduct, which includes a total respect for the human and democratic rights of its citizens. To date, its record has been found lamentably wanting.

EPILOGUE

In the light of the brutal events which took place in China in the summer of 1989, it is difficult to evaluate the past forty years of Communist rule with complete objectivity. However, one must still attempt to weigh the record in the balance, and decide how successful China's leaders have been in raising the standard of living of their people, and how far that should be the criterion of success. Because the leaders of the Chinese Communist Party have regularly visited oppression and catastrophe on their people, one is in danger of denying them even their incontrovertible successes.

Looked at in bald economic terms, China can boast considerable success. When the Communists took over in 1949 China had a population of 540 million. It produced only one million tons of steel, and 111 million tons of grain. Years of war had brought its industrial growth to a halt. In 1988, its population having doubled over four decades, China produced 59 million tons of steel and 394 million tons of grain. Since 1949 its economic growth rate has been one of the fastest in the world. Over the past decade, with an annual growth rate of 10 per cent, it has been *the* fastest growing. However, critics of China's economic growth rate point out that although South Korea started from an equally low point after the Korean War, it is already far ahead of China economically, because it was not subjected to endless, destructive political campaigns. Furthermore, the pattern of development in China has been very uneven, with huge imbalances in agriculture and industry which more consistent policies would have obviated. One is still witnessing an inability to make sensible investment decisions, either by state planning or by market forces.

Apart from the truly disastrous years of the Great Leap Forward, China can boast that it has managed to feed and clothe a quarter of the world's population. But as China's leaders admit, and as one can see for oneself in some of the less accessible areas of the country, food is meagre in the extreme. As discussed in Chapter 5, China has an impressive record in the control of disease and infant mortality, and its citizens now live for as long as those in much more developed countries. This is bringing its own problems, and in the next century China will face the nightmare problem of how to provide social security for hundreds of millions of old people.

With a per capita GNP of only US $350 per annum, China is one of the world's poorest nations. Yet the economic reforms have at least doubled, and in many cases trebled or quadrupled the incomes of millions of Chinese peasants and industrial workers. However, the undoubted improvement in the standard of living has been partially offset by inflation, spiralling prices and the other problems of an overheating economy.

Where does China go next? The events of June have forced a complete reappraisal of China's way forward over the next decade. There are at least three possible scenarios. Two of these are directly predicated on the death of Deng Xiaoping. He is now 85 years old, and is physically very frail, following a major operation at the end of 1988. At present it is Deng who is just managing to hold together an extremely uneasy leadership coalition, in which the younger hardliners resent the re-emergence of the old hardliners. A worst-case scenario is that when Deng dies there will be a vicious scramble to see who can grab power. An equally hardline group of younger men would take over. In China, as elsewhere, hardline conservatism is not limited to the old, and is just as likely to be found amongst the middle-aged and the young.

If this were to happen, the prospects for China would be bleak. The leadership would turn its face against democratic reforms and continue its harsh repression of the student movement. Although the leaders would continue to talk of economic reforms, and of opening up to the outside world, these reforms would lack the bold liberalisation which is so vital if they are truly to change the Chinese economy. As has already been shown, China's economic reforms were able to get so far and no further because the government lacked the courage to cast off the more constricting ties of socialist central planning.

One understands any government's fear of social disorder in the wake of inflation and price rises, but economic reforms will never truly take off unless people are prepared to grit their teeth for a few years, and accept that these are the unpleasant side of real reform.

If a truly hardline government persists in China with all the attendant dangers of increased xenophobia, there is a possibility that there will be considerably less foreign investment in China, and fewer foreign credits. Overseas Chinese will cut back on their vital investments in south China. Should this happen then the economy will stagnate and China will be unable to service its foreign debt. It will have to cut down on imports, and this will lead to further discontent amongst the population. This will then fuel another cycle of repression, with more and more agitators and dissenters incarcerated in labour camps in the inhospitable regions of Xinjiang and Qinghai.

And this is where the PLA might play a greater role. One has to say that we really do not know exactly where their loyalties lie. As an army, they obey orders, but there are indications that many soldiers were very unhappy about the events in Tiananmen Square. The PLA must recognise that for those who know the truth about the massacre, the relationship between themselves and the people will never be the same again. If the country continues in a state of sullen unrest, the army will have to play a greater role in controlling that unrest. There is no reason to suppose that they would enjoy the role of policing their own people, when they should be training as modern soldiers to fight any possible external enemy. Whilst there is some evidence that one section of the PLA would like to have a greater say in the political affairs of the country, it is probably true that the majority feel that a professional army should be just that, and should not revert to the kind of powerful political role which it had at the end of the Cultural Revolution.

Another factor which must be taken into account is that the

PLA (the army itself numbers only some 2.3 million, with the navy and the air force taking the numbers up to 3 million) would have great difficulty controlling a truly rebellious urban population of some 200 million, even with the help of the People's Armed Police. The situation is now exacerbated by the millions of itinerant workers who are a potential factor of social unrest. Should the situation get quite out of hand, one cannot rule out the possibility that the military would act as kingmakers and put in a set of leaders who would be more acceptable to the people. In return, the PLA would expect an increase in the military budget, and possibly greater representation on the Politburo and the Central Committee.

A more optimistic scenario is that on Deng's death the country might be in such an unhappy economic state that the liberal economic reformers would take power with a mandate from the PLA and the Communist Party and move China further on the path of economic reform which Zhao Ziyang promoted before his fall from grace.

We would then expect to see the kind of dynamic growth and gradual liberalisation characteristic of the best years of the 1979–89 reforms. There would be greater political liberalisation, with multi-candidate elections at increasingly high levels of government. The economy would continue to move further towards market forces, and all the problems that would entail, and there would be greater diversification of the means of ownership. The state would own progressively less of the means of production and distribution, and the collective and the private sector would own progressively more.

One would see more and more young technocrats, many of whom had been trained abroad, move into high places. If that were to happen many of the brightest and best, who are at present reluctant to return to a China where they would be under-utilised at best, and persecuted at worst, would return to give their services to their country.

In such a situation the all-devouring power of the Communist Party would slowly lessen. One would see the growth of more powerful opposition voices, as in the Soviet Union. The National People's Congress, China's the highest legislative body, would therefore be more truly representative and a sterner critic of government. Such a state of affairs would once again make China acceptable to the West. However, such a scenario presupposes that the Chinese Communist Party is capable of radically reforming itself, of which I have grave doubts.

Having offered these possible blueprints for the future, there is at least one more. The Tiananmen Square Massacre has gravely damaged China's reputation as a country genuinely trying to modernise, both in the eyes of the outside world and of its own people. The confidence of the Chinese people, so devastated by the Cultural Revolution and indeed by all the previous political campaigns, was being slowly restored by more than a decade of peaceful progress. Now, once again, the Ministry of Truth in all its Orwellian power is lying to the people and terrorising them into submission. At present, and probably for some time to come, people will be too stunned to think of taking any action of their own against the government, and will merely hope to lead their lives without being too conspicuous.

But I feel that there are grounds for optimism, because the people of China have seen that there are alternatives to lies and suppression. Even before the decade of reforms started they knew that there were political alternatives, and the pro-democracy movements in China since 1978 have reinforced that belief. They know that even in the Eastern Bloc some countries are moving fast towards a greater degree of political plurality. They know that the world is changing, and that there is an inexorable historical move against authoritarian regimes.

It is true that the people who are aware of the changing world certainly do not make up anything like the majority of the Chinese population. But it is also true that it is minorities who generally set about changing the political face of a country. It was the small intellectual elite of the Chinese Communist Party who eventually infected the Chinese peasantry with a desire to overthrow the old order in 1949. Although one could not now plead starvation and widespread physical oppression as reasons to drum up support against the present Chinese government, one could certainly say that many sectors of the Chinese hierarchy are as corrupt as were the Kuomintang. Once a country has basically fulfilled the material needs of its people, then they begin to want freedom from political suppression. They begin to realise that man is a repository of spiritual as well as material needs. Since the Chinese Communist Party can no longer satisfy those spiritual needs something else will have to take its place.

At this stage it is difficult to see what that might be. One hopes that there would be a natural trend towards a more democratic society, with a more pluralist approach to both economics and politics. If China is to become the economic giant of the twenty-first century which its leaders want and its neighbours fear, then it must cast off its present cautious attitude to reform.

There is one inescapable truth. Whatever happens, there are no easy solutions for China. The country is too big and too poor. Even with a stable and enlightened government, progress will always be beset with problems. At present the government is neither. Whoever takes over the reins from the present leaders will have an appallingly difficult and unenviable task ahead.

INDEX

4 May 1919 Movement, 152–3
7 May Cadre Schools, 81
16 May Circular, 54
Afghanistan, 188, 192
Afro-Asian Solidarity Organisation, 181
agriculture, 32–5, 44–8, 104, 109–10, 117–19, 132, 171–2, 202
Anti-Rightist Campaign, 5, 35, 37–8

Bandung Line, 170
Big Character Posters, 55, 57
Britain, and China, 78, 167, 181, 189; and Hong Kong, 197–8

Cambodia, 187, 192, 193–4
Central Committee, Ninth Congress, 84
Chen Boda, 84–6
Chen Yun, 42, 126, 161
Chiang Kai-shek, 9–10, 23–4, 27
China, attitude to war, 185; and balance of power, 172; border with Soviet Union, 180, 182; coast/inland differences, 131–2; counties, 150; future leadership, 202–4; importance of numbers, 38–9; international relations see name of country; minorities, 177–8; proposed partition, 26
Chinese People's Volunteers, 168
class structure, 31, 33, 61, 90
communes, 33, 39–41, 104, 117–118, 131
Communist Party, 8–11, 95–6, 135, 150–1, 157–9
Communist Revolution, 17–19
Confucius, 96–7
Cultural Revolution, 5, 52–86, 93–5

Dazhai Brigade, 110
Democracy Wall, 136, 145–6
Deng Xiaoping, 5, 10, 97, 109, 112, 115, 202; and Great Leap Forward, 42–3; and international relations, 174–5, 183, 188, 193; and Mao, 113, 115; reforms, 19, 116; retirement from Politburo, 126; return to power, 95, 99; and the Second Revolution, 112; and Tiananmen Incident, 100; and Tiananmen Square 1989, 153–4, 161
economics, 5, 30–1, 124–8, 131–2, 134, 201–3; and foreign trade, 183–4, 186, 203; private enterprise, 122–5, 129–30, 133; social effects, 116, 119, 124–6, 128–31
education, 52, 55, 62–3, 80–1, 90–1

Fang Lizhi, 38, 147, 150, 189
Fifth Modernisation, 145
Five Principles of Peaceful Coexistence, 170
Five Year Plans, 30
Five-Antis Campaign, 31
foreign investment and trade, 183–4, 186, 203
foreign policy and see international relations, name of country, 85, 91, 164–200
Four Cardinal Principles, 146
Four Modernisations, 116, 145
Four Olds, 59–60

Gang of Four, 5, 50, 99, 107–10
Gorbachev, Mikhail, 194–5
Great Leap Forward, 5, 35, 39–42 46–7, 49–50, 174

Hainan, 128–9
Han Chinese in Tibet, 177–8
Hong Kong, 78, 196–7
Hu Yaobang, 5, 148, 152
Hua Guofeng, 89, 99, 106–7, 115–16, 188; as leader, 111
human rights, 135, 159–60
Hundred Flowers Movement, 5, 35–6, 171–2

India, 170, 175–6, 179–80, 190–1
industrial development, 30, 121–2, 130–1
INF Treaty, 192
international relations and see foreign policy, name of country, 78–9, 180–2, 189–90, 199–200

Japan, 23–5, 184–6
Jiang Qing, 14–15, 50, 59, 79, 93–4, 107–9

Kang Sheng, 50, 84
Kissinger, Henry, 89, 183
KMT (Nationalist Army), 9–10, 17, 20–1, 24, 26–7
Korea, North, 196
Korea, South, 196, 201
Korean War, 5, 30, 167–9
Krushchev, Nikita, 41, 46, 167, 169–74

land distribution, 18, 32–3, 91, 118
legal system, 108, 145–6
Li Peng, 148, 155, 158, 161
Lin Biao, 5, 17, 57; and the army, 50, 79; discreditation, 85–6, 94, 95, 97
Lin Biao Affair, 86, 87–9
Little Red Book, 50

INDEX

Little Red Devils, 20
Liu Binyan, 38, 147
Liu Shaoqi, 34, 56–7, 83–4
Long March, 20–2

Macao, 196
MacMahon Line, 175
Mao Zedong, 5, 6–7, 8–15, 87–8, 101, 103–4, 106; and atom bomb, 172; and betrayal, 95–6; and collectivisation, 41; and the Cultural Revolution, 52, 54; and Deng Xiaoping, 113, 115; disappearances, 56; foreign policy, 165–7; and Gang of Four, 107, 109; and Great Leap Forward, 49–51; and Korean War, 168; and Kruschev, 41, 167, 169–74; and leadership, 22, 75, 103–5; and military power, 85; nostalgia for, 151; personality cult, 58; and PLA, 89; politics of, 103, 167; and Red Guards, 79–81; and Soviet Union, 179–80; and Stalin, 166, 169; works of, 50, 58; Yangtse river swim, 56–7; and Zhou Enlai, 101–4
Million Heroes Army, 76
Mongolia, 192, 194

Nanjing, 24
National Peoples Congress, 98, 150
Nationalists (KMT), 9–10, 17, 20–1, 24, 26–7
Nien Cheng, 61–2
Nixon, Richard, 183
nuclear capability, 38, 42, 171–2, 173, 179, 180

Party Congresses, Eighth, 34
Peng Dehuai, 10, 42, 45–6, 174
Peng Zhen, 54, 126, 161
People's Daily, 91, 149
Peoples Liberation Army (PLA), 19, 51, 84, 89, 203–4; and Cultural Revolution, 75–7; and Tiananmen Square, 154–5, 163
population, 47–8, 120–1, 201–2
Provincial Party Committees, 89

Qian Qichen, 193
Qing Dynasty, 7, 176
Quemoy, 172–3

Red Army, 19–22, 24–7
Red Guards, 58–64, 74, 76–8, 79–80
Republic, foundation of, 5
Revolutionary Committees, 75

Second Revolution, 112

Shanghai, military importance, 98–9
Shanghai Commune, 74–5
Shanghai Communique, 183
Sino-Soviet Treaty of Friendship, Alliance and Mutual Assistance, 166, 169–70
Soviet Union, border with China, 85, 180, 182, 191–4; financial aid, 166; military aid, 168–9, 191; military presence in SE Asia, 194–5; political contact, 5, 25–6, 45–6, 154, 164–7, 169–73, 179–81, 188, 191–5; technical aid, 45–6, 165, 174, 193; trade relations, 169–70; and United States, 173–4
Stalin, 25–6, 166, 169
steel production, 41, 43–4, 201
student uprisings *and see* Tiananmen Square 1989, 136, 145, 147–8
Sun Yat-sen, 7–8, 9

Taiwan, 10, 172–3, 198–9
Tangshan earthquake, 101
Thought Reform, 31–2
Three-Antis Campaign, 31
Tiananmen Incident, 100–1
Tiananmen Square 1949, 5, 58
Tiananmen Square 1989, 5 6, 152–63, 189–90
Tibet, 45, 60, 170, 175–8

United States, and China, 25, 164–5, 170, 172–3, 188–90; and Korean War, 168–9; and Soviet Union, 173–4

Vietnam, 85, 180, 187–8

Wang Guangmei, 34, 73, 82
Wang Hongwen, 74, 96, 107–8
Wei Jingsheng, 145–6
Work Teams, 73, 80
Wu Han, 51, 53

Xiafang, 37–8
Xi'an Incident, 23

Yalta Agreement, 26
Yanan, 22
Yao Wenyuan, 51, 53, 74–5, 107

Zhang Chunqiao, 50, 74–5,107–8
Zhao Ziyang, 122, 148–50, 155
Zhou Enlai, 5, 9–10, 15–17, 97–103; in Africa, 180–1; and Cultural Revolution, 76; foreign policy, 170; and Mao, 101–3
Zhou-Nixon Communique, 183
Zhu De, 10, 101